Writing Handbooks

Writing
for Radio

Books in the 'Writing Handbooks' series

Freelance Writing for Newspapers • Jill Dick

The Writer's Rights • Michael Legat

Writing for Children • Margaret Clark

Writing Crime Fiction • H.R.F. Keating

Writing Erotic Fiction • Derek Parker

Writing about Food • Jenny Linford

Writing Fantasy Fiction • Sarah LeFanu

Writing Historical Fiction • Rhona Martin

Writing Horror Fiction • Guy N. Smith

Writing for Magazines • Jill Dick

Writing a Play • Steve Gooch

Writing Popular Fiction • Rona Randall

Writing for Radio • Rosemary Horstmann

Writing for the Teenage Market • Ann de Gale

Writing for Television • Gerald Kelsey

Writing a Thriller • André Jute

Writing about Travel • Morag Campbell

Other books for writers

Writers' and Artists' Yearbook

Word Power: a guide to creative writing • Julian Birkett

Research for Writers • Ann Hoffmann

Interviewing Techniques for Writers and
Researchers • Susan Dunne

Writing Handbooks

Writing for Radio

THIRD EDITION

Rosemary Horstmann

A & C Black • London

Third edition 1997
First edition 1988
Second edition 1991

A & C Black (Publishers) Limited
35 Bedford Row, London WC1R 4JH

© 1997, 1988, 1991 Rosemary Horstmann

0–7136–4649–7

A CIP catalogue record for this book is available from
the British Library.

Typeset in 10½ on 12½ pt Sabon
Printed and bound in Great Britain by
Creative Print and Design (Wales), Ebbw Vale

Contents

Introduction to the Third Edition

In the ten years since this book was first published a multitude of changes have taken place in the broadcasting world. These changes have been both in the organisation of the different bodies involved, and in the technological developments of which they now have to take account.

We have seen two new Broadcasting Acts, in 1990 and 1996. These have brought with them the disappearance of the IBA and its replacement by a separate Radio Authority and Independent Television Commission, a huge expansion in the numbers of Independent Local Radio stations, and the arrival of three commercially funded national radio networks – Classic FM, Virgin 1215 and Talk Radio. In addition, the BBC has announced a fundamental and controversial reorganisation of the whole of its operation. The question 'Can more mean better, or must it mean worse?' is still being hotly debated, and the jury is still out.

The future of radio in Britain lies in the hands of aspiring writers and broadcasters now coming onto the airwaves. There is a marked trend towards 'multi-skilling', and the term 'convergence' is being bandied about more and more freely. This means that the true professional will be capable of working in more than one medium. If you can write and broadcast your own material, record interviews and edit them yourself, create programmes for both radio and television, your future is much brighter than if you see yourself as a radio-writer only. However, it is a great mistake to confuse the media – radio is much more than television without the pictures. The arrival of new audio visual technologies such as CD-ROM are drawing the worlds of broadcasting and publishing closer together. Anyone looking for a career in either of these areas should be fully aware of developments in the other. Audio publishing is taking off, and skills acquired as a radio writer can be put to good use in this field. The other big development is the digital revolution. You will find more about this in Chapter 4, but one clear signal is that the ability to use a computer and a mouse will be a vital part of a professional broadcaster's skills in the future.

Radio is a branch of the entertainment industry. Would-be professionals should appreciate that broadcasters fall into two main categories: those who plan or produce programmes and so commission writers and performers, and those who do the writing and performing. People in the first category tend to hold staff appointments or long-term contracts; those in the second are almost invariably freelances. The salaried producer or executive may count on a steady job with a pay check at the end of the month; on the other hand he/she will seldom be heard, and as far as the public is concerned, remain largely anonymous. The producer is an *eminence grise* behind the scenes, holding the purse strings and dispensing patronage.

The life of the freelance is more glamorous and more chancey. A successful radio personality can make an international name. But there is no job security. The freelance is always dependent on the goodwill of those who control the broadcasting machine to keep the commissions coming. Schedules alter, producers move, tastes change. It is a truism of the freelance life that you are either overworked or starving.

What is a producer? He – or she – is an ideas merchant. The producer's job is to fill air time in a way which will attract listeners; to buy talent, in the form of writers and performers, and work with them to develop and polish their creative efforts. In film and television the functions of producer and director are divided, but in radio producers are usually their own directors. This means that, having commissioned or bought scripts and chosen the performers they then go into the studio and direct the programmes, live or recorded. Producers have to know the audience they are trying to reach, understand the medium of radio, and help broadcasters to present themselves and their material as effectively as possible.

There are other tasks in broadcasting besides producing and performing. Every station has engineers, administrators and accountants. If it is a commercial station it will have a sales section. Depending on the scale of the operation, there will be secretaries, telephonists, perhaps a librarian, certainly press and public relations staff. If you are drawn to this crazy stimulating world, one way in is to get yourself a job – any job – at a radio station in order to watch the wheels go round, make contacts, and convince people that you are genuine in your determination to break into the competitive business of broadcasting. If you have taken a hand in school or college productions or helped with a hospital broadcasting station this will stand you in good stead.

It is hard to make a living as a freelance, especially in the early stages. Any writer needs to find a way of keeping body and soul together while working at his creative calling in leisure hours, until he becomes sufficiently well-established to be able to give up the day-job and write full time. The most valuable quality to cultivate is thick-skinned persistence. If your early efforts meet with failure, analyse the reasons and keep trying. I hope this book will help, and that eventually you will win through to the ultimate reward – being paid for what you most enjoy doing.

1. The Nature of Radio

Radio has been with us since the beginning of the twentieth century. In Britain the first regular service of radio programmes for the general public was started in 1922. Many things have changed since then. I can remember my grandfather sitting with headphones over his ears beside an enormous and mysterious black box with glowing glass bulbs on top. What he was listening to I never knew. Perhaps it was one of Sir Walford Davies's early talks on music; it might even have been the first radio play, broadcast in 1924. Whatever it was, the signal reached his receiver, with its glimmering valves, by means of a wire which led out of the window and across the garden to the top of a tall flagpole. This elaborate aerial array was an essential part of the paraphernalia. The ritual of Grandpa listening to the wireless had more than a touch of the ceremonial, like some arcane religious observance. Woe betide us children if our clumsy footsteps should shake the delicate connections or disturb the fine tuning. Once while he was sitting rapt in some communication from the unknown my two-year-old sister delt Grandpa a smart blow on his bald head with a walking stick. He leapt to his feet convinced the set had been struck by lightning.

The pole at the bottom of the garden disappeared long ago, but headphones, having ceased to be essential, have now made a comeback as part of the new mobility of radio. Today people no longer have to sit beside the receiver. Liberated by new technology from the tyranny of trailing cables they can listen to the American President addressing a press conference in the White House as they ride to work in the train, or enjoy their favourite pop programme as they jog round the park. This universal accessibility makes radio unique as a means of communication.

Since the 1940s television has gradually taken over the limelight. Television is expensive, sensational, glamorous. But radio remains a highly significant element in the world's mass media. Although it no longer makes headlines, even in a television-rich country like Britain there are few who do not listen to the radio at least once a day, and a shut-down in radio services would bring far more universal consternation than a shut-down in television.

Radio is cheap. It can span vast distances in the twinkling of an eye, and because, unlike television, it does not demand a reliable mains electricity supply it can be used with confidence to reach isolated communities and individuals beyond the range of piped power, whether in remote moorland farmsteads, in ships at sea, or the Australian outback. Indeed, the latest contribution to receiver technology is the development of a clockwork radio, which does not even depend on batteries to power it. Here we come to the first significant point for the writer to remember about radio broadcasting.

We call it a mass medium, and it is true that radio audiences are counted in millions. But they are millions of individuals, sitting in ones and twos by their own firesides, or listening in their cars or out on their farms and cattle-stations. The style in which they like to be addressed is an intimate one, not at all the same manner as they would expect at a public meeting. The broadcaster is only as far from the audience as his mouth is from the microphone and the listener's chair is from the loud-speaker at the other end.

The second important point is, that the listener is for all practical purposes blind. The broadcaster's message must be conveyed through one sense only, the sense of hearing. This is not to say that the contributions to total experience made by the other four senses should be ignored. Rather, these contributions must cunningly be incorporated in the broadcaster's work. Choice of the right words will enable the listener to see, touch, smell and even taste – in imagination. It is this skill of stimulating the imagination that lies at the heart of the radio-broadcaster's art.

The ordinary writer starts with a sheet of blank paper; the broadcaster starts with silence. Every sound that is added to that silence will carry some clue, which the audience will be waiting, all ears, to interpret. The very quality of the acoustic will convey something of the location in which words are spoken. A religious service relayed from a cathedral sounds quite different from a studio broadcast. Practitioners of radio drama know well how to exploit these subtleties, and an accompaniment of exotic background noises adds an invaluable touch of authenticity to news reports from remote corners of the earth.

Thirdly, the broadcaster must never forget that listeners are bound to take in the message sequentially, in the order in which they receive it. If they do not immediately understand what has been said, they cannot look back to the beginning of the paragraph, or reread the previous page as one can with print. For most listeners the first hearing is the last, and anything misunderstood or missed is gone forever. Hence, it is essential for the speaker to structure the message carefully with this limitation in mind, and to have a clear mental image of the people for whom the broadcast is intended.

The key points made in this chapter are valid for every type of radio programme, and should never be forgotten. Radio is an intimate medium, carrying its message to millions of individuals through their ears alone. Listeners have to accept broadcast information in the sequence in which it is presented. Clarity of thought and empathy with the audience are the marks of the successful broadcaster.

2. The History of British Broadcasting

It has been said that world broadcasting falls into three main categories: permissive – you give the public what it likes; paternalistic – you give it what you think it ought to like; and authoritarian – you give it what the government likes. The last category manifests itself in totalitarian regimes. The second is typified by the BBC output in Britain, and the first by the commercial approach largely adopted by Independent Radio stations in this country and pioneered by American radio. In the USA radio, and later television, have always been regarded as part of the business system, to be financed by revenue from advertising and sponsorship. Only comparatively recently has a need been recognised for public service broadcasting as an alternative to the commercial services. The early 1920s saw a free-for-all boom in American radio that led to chaos on the airwaves, and it was primarily this rather than distaste for advertising that led the British government to insist on strict regulation and, for the first fifty years, no advertising.

The BBC and the birth of British broadcasting

Broadcasting in Britain started with the BBC. The British Broadcasting Company developed into the British Broadcasting Corporation, which received a Royal Charter in 1927. Its first Director General, John Reith (later Lord Reith), was a visionary of towering personality and unswerving rectitude. He believed that the BBC had a duty to inform, educate and entertain its audience to the highest standards. Under his guidance a tradition of public service broadcasting was created against which all later developments have come to be measured.

The BBC was given a monopoly of the British airwaves. It was to be financed by a licence fee paid by the audience, and was forbidden to accept money for advertising. The Monarch in Council was to appoint a Board of Governors, who would in turn appoint a Director General responsible to them for the running of the Corporation. Subject to the law of the land, the BBC was to be free of detailed control over the content of its programmes. The Government would, however, retain a right of veto over the broadcasting of any material which was felt to be against the national interest, and the BBC could also be required to broadcast official announcements. The BBC would have the right to state when it was making a broadcast at the request of the Government. In 1937, when the first Royal Charter was renewed, the BBC was given responsibility for television as well as radio, and also authorised to broadcast 'for the benefit of Our dominions beyond the seas and territories under Our protection.' This was the Empire Service, which later became the BBC World Service.

The Fourth Charter was granted in 1952. The Government had 'come to the conclusion that in the expanding field of television provision should be made to permit some element of competition.' Accordingly, the BBC's licence to broadcast was for the first time described as 'non-exclusive'. This paved the way for the breaking of the BBC's monopoly with the launching of Independent Television, later to be joined by Independent Radio. It is now more than seventy years since the granting of the BBC's first Royal Charter and Licence. In that time the BBC has done its best to guard its independence from Government control. Its policy of impartiality and objectivity in the handling of news and controversial issues has brought it a world-wide reputation which British governments of all political colours have regarded as a national asset. The Corporation has acted responsibly so that the government until recently never felt compelled to invoke its power of veto. Then, for a time, there was an official ban on broadcasting the actual voices of members of the IRA. The BBC exercised its right to state that, in accordance with the Government ruling, words of IRA members were being spoken by actors. Other countries find it hard to believe that the BBC is truly independent, and indeed the Corporation walks a delicate tightrope in its handling of news and current affairs. Nevertheless, anything that looks like an attempt by the government of the day to interfere in BBC output is greeted with storms of indignation in Parliament and the press, where the BBC is hotly defended as a flagship of free speech.

A new look BBC

On May 1, 1996 the BBC's seventh Royal Charter came into force. The following month, as the latest Broadcasting Bill was being finalised in Parliament, the BBC announced a wholesale structural reorganisation. To be put in place by April 1, 1997 is a downsized Corporation consisting of six units: BBC Broadcast, BBC Production, BBC News, BBC Worldwide, BBC Resources, and the Corporate Centre. Key features of the new dispensation are:

1) the separation of broadcasting from production
2) the integration of radio and television, and
3) the concentration of BBC operations at White City, away from the old BBC headquarters at Broadcasting House.

The diagram on page 10 shows an outline of this reorganisation. Notice that all domestic radio channels except 5 Live become the responsibility of the Director of Radio under the aegis of BBC Broadcast. Radio 5 Live, however, comes under BBC News, and World Service radio comes under BBC Worldwide.

It is not yet clear how many aspects of this controversial scheme will work in practice. Plans for World Service Radio have aroused anxiety, particularly at the Foreign Office, by which the service is financed. A joint Foreign Office/BBC working group is being established to oversee effects that the changes may have on the ethos and operation of the World Service.

BBC domestic services

The Broadcasting Act of 1990 put an end to the practice of 'simulcasting' (broadcasting the same output on more than one frequency), and this forced the BBC to undertake a fundamental reorganisation of its domestic programming. It now has five national networks – Radios 1, 2 and 3 transmitting on VHF, Radio 4 transmitting on VHF and Long Wave, and Radio 5

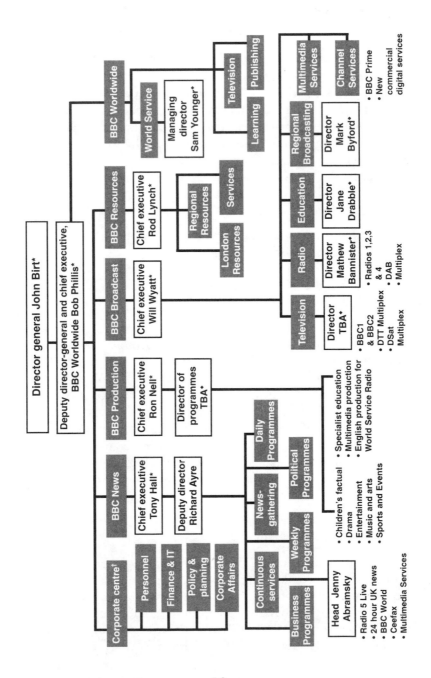

Live transmitting on Medium Wave only. Each of these net-works has an individual character and is designed to appeal to a specific section of the audience.

Radio 1 FM has established an image as the channel for young adult listeners. It attracts an audience mainly in the age-range 15–34, with pop music, DJ chat, snappily presented news, comedy programmes, documentaries and drama, with some social action campaigning.

Radio 2 FM is regarded as easy listening for the over-50s. With a backbone of music, much of it live, more than a third of its broadcasts consist of speech, covering documentaries, religion, news, current affairs, arts, entertainment and comedy. There is a fair leavening of nostalgia.

Radio 3 FM is the BBC's premier cultural service on radio with a core of quality music and drama, and an audience at the upper end of the age range. It is the nation's major patron of classical music.

Radio 4 FM *and* LW is considered as the nation's primary information and speech network, and draws an adult audience of all ages. Its two frequencies are sometimes split to accommodate different programmes; for example live cricket commentaries and Open University programmes go out on the long wave channel while the regular output continues on FM.

Radio 5 Live is the youngest of the networks, and was first launched in August 1990 as a channel for children, schools and sport. It was relaunched in 1994 for news and sport only. This has meant squeezing school broadcasts into the Radio 3 schedule, and making space for some children's entertainment programmes on Radio 4.

Programmes may be contributed to these main networks by producers working in any of the BBC's regional production centres. Transmitters in the regions – especially the three national regions, Wales, Scotland and Northern Ireland – are able to opt out of the main Radio 4 network to broadcast programmes of their own.

In addition to its five main networks broadcasting nation-wide, the BBC also has thirty eight Local Radio stations. These are stations with limited-power transmitters designed to serve the particular needs and interests of listeners living in their immediate areas.

All the BBC's domestic services are paid for from the television licence fee. There is no separate licence for radio sets. Nearly two thirds of the UK population listen to BBC radio at some time during the week.

Radio in the Commonwealth

The British way of broadcasting was growing up at the same time as the British Empire was dissolving. One by one the colonies became independent nations, and imperial bonds were transmuted into the looser links of Commonwealth. As the patches of red drained from the map and the Empire builders withdrew they left behind many legacies, of which two concern this book. The English language became a world *lingua franca* through which people living in scattered communities who spoke different languages – and different dialects of the same language – could talk to each other and be understood. The second legacy was the idea of broadcasting as a public service. Even where commercial radio and television have come to exist side by side with a national service, as they have in Britain, this concept continues to permeate broadcasting throughout the former British Empire.

All India Radio from its headquarters in New Delhi operates a broadcasting network of 164 centres, covering all the important cultural and linguistic regions of that vast subcontinent. Its programmes consist of news, music, talks, plays, discussions, interviews, special programmes for women and children, schools and universities, and rural broadcasts for community listening. All India Radio is a department of the Ministry of Information and Broadcasting, and is funded nationally. It has all the characteristics of an Asian BBC. A commercial radio service was introduced in 1967 from AIR Bombay-Pune-Nagpur, and this has now been considerably extended.

In Africa, broadcasting holds a position of overwhelming importance among the public media. Radio, above all, is the only medium which can overcome the barriers of illiteracy, distance, and lack of transportation. The trend in Africa has been towards the authoritarian pattern, and in spite of high ideals on the part of individuals, broadcasting tends to be under direct government control and closely involved with politics.

The overthrow of the apartheid system in South Africa, however, should bring a flowering of creativity among would be radio-writers who have hitherto been unable to present their ideas on the air.

BBC worldwide

In the spring of 1994 the BBC reshaped the structure of its international and commercial activities under the title of BBC Worldwide, with a board chaired by the Deputy Director-General. These operations are now organised into three separate directorates: BBC World Service, providing the BBC's international radio services and news programming for World Service Television; BBC International Television, and BBC Publishing, taking responsibility for books, videos, magazines and licensing.

The directorate which concerns this book is the BBC World Service, which has an average weekly radio audience of 130 million. Amongst the audience for major international radio broadcasters worldwide, more than 80% listen to the World Service. The BBC broadcasts in English 24 hours a day. In addition, news and current affairs coverage is transmitted in a range of foreign tongues which have included more than fifty different languages since the service started in 1938.

The headquarters of the BBC World Service, at Bush House in London, is a miniature BBC in itself. It has a similar range of departments, and although it takes a good deal of material from the BBC's domestic services freelancers should remember that it also originates many programmes itself, specially designed for its overseas audiences. The emphasis in the World Service output is on accurate and unbiased news and information, projection of British culture, and education. 'English by Radio' has been an overwhelming success, and BBC English teaching programmes are heard or seen all over the world.

The World Service is responsible also for the Monitoring Service, based at Caversham near Reading, where foreign radio broadcasts are listened to and reported. The BBC World Service is paid for by Government Grant in Aid and draws no finance from the licence fee. More than 80 other countries support broadcasting services addressed to listeners outside their national boundaries.

Commercial radio in Britain

The BBC monopoly was challenged from the start by Radio Normandy and Radio Luxembourg, commercial stations broadcasting from the continent of Europe. Radio Normandy did not survive the Second World War, and Radio Luxembourg has also now ceased. In the 1960s the assault on British airwaves was continued by 'pirate' radio stations such as Radio Caroline, operating from a ship in the Thames Estuary, and offering a diet of pop music and disc-jockey chat. Clearly there was a demand for different sorts of radio, and in 1973 the first legitimate commercial stations were launched in mainland Britain. The Independent Television Authority was renamed the Independent Broadcasting Authority and given responsibility for overseeing commercial radio.

The advent of advertising was strictly regulated. Applicants for franchises had to convince the IBA that their programme plans would provide an acceptable standard of service for each local community involved. It was forbidden to integrate advertising into programme content, and the commercials themselves were to be clearly segregated. Sponsorship was forbidden except under the strictest rules.

The 1990 Broadcasting Act and after

The 1990 Broadcasting Act changed the landscape for both radio and television. The IBA was superseded by two separate organisations, the Independent Television Commission, and the Radio Authority.

The Radio Authority acts as a licensing and regulatory body for sound broadcasting services in the United Kingdom other than those provided by the BBC. It has a Chairman, Deputy Chairman and between four and ten other members, all appointed by the Government. The Authority may grant licences for both national and local services. Regarding national services, the Act stipulates that one of these must be of predominantly spoken word material, and another a service which consists mainly of music 'other than pop'.

The Radio Authority may also grant Restricted Service Licences. These are usually for a maximum duration of 28 days,

14

and for a limited geographical coverage (coverage of a town, or approximately a two-mile radius in a city). They are granted for a wide range of reasons, broadly falling into two categories: coverage of special events – for example a festival or carnival – and trial or experimental services.

The emphasis in the Act is on the provision of a wide range and diversity of services calculated to appeal to a variety of tastes and interests. Stress is also laid on fair and effective competition in the provision of independent broadcasting services. Many of the previous restrictions on advertising and sponsorship have been swept away and the Radio Authority is enjoined to exercise its regulatory function with a light hand.

There must still be a clear separation between the advertisements and the programmes. Presenters are not allowed to advertise products on their shows; children's and religious programmes are protected from unsuitable advertisements, and sponsors must not be the suppliers of any product unsuitable for advertising on the air.

Since the passing of the Broadcasting Act there has been an explosion of independent radio in the country. There are now more than 150 local commercial stations, and 3 national channels. Classic FM went on air on September 7, 1992 with a diet of classical music which provides competition for BBC Radio 3; Richard Branson's Virgin 1215 followed on April 30, 1993, and is now attempting to rival BBC Radio 1 FM in the pop field. The third national independent radio channel is Talk FM, which went on the air in February 1995.

The Broadcasting Act also required the BBC to buy in programmes from independent producers, and this, together with all the other developments, has led to an expansion of opportunities on the creative side of the radio industry.

Commercial radio stations are no longer required by law to include a strand of public service programming in their output, and do not even have to carry regular news bulletins unless they decide to do so. Traditions in this field, however, are very strong, and many of them continue in response to audience expectation.

Independent Radio News provides a news service in which standards of balance, accuracy and impartiality are scrupulously maintained. This is available to all independent stations if they choose to use it.

15

British forces broadcasting service

This is the radio arm of the Services Sound and Vision Corporation. Its role is to provide a service for the British forces overseas, encompassing entertainment, information and education, together with a link with home. BFBS operates stations in Germany, Cyprus, Gibraltar, Hong Kong, Brunei, the Falklands and Belize, which devise their own programme schedules to suit the needs and interests of their audiences, drawing on local contributions as well as material supplied by London. BFBS HQ broadcasts live from London, and records over 50 hours of programming every week in a wide range of speech and music. This is syndicated to overseas stations. In addition, up to thirty Royal Navy ships at sea regularly receive a large proportion of BFBS London's output every week. Recently, satellite transmission has made it possible to hook up direct with all the main overseas BFBS stations, and broadcast 24 hours a day, with up-to-date news on the hour, and sometimes the half-hour as well. Sports commentaries are particularly appreciated by the service audience overseas. The Services Sound and Vision Corporation is a registered charity, and any profits are split 50/50 between improving the service and the various benevolent funds. A special agreement on copyright has been negotiated with the Performing Rights Society, on condition that none of the BFBS output is ever heard in Britain.

Into the future

With the passing of the 1996 Broadcasting Act the BBC appears secure into the next century. The BBC Charter has been renewed for another ten years, and the licence fee is to remain as its principal source of funding. It is clear, however, that the BBC is now operating in a world of increasing competition, both artistic and financial. In 1994 the *Guardian* newspaper commented in a leading article that the BBC required 'Ten more years that need to be glorious.' It is up to the writers and artists who work in broadcasting to see that this is achieved.

3. Writing for Speech

The crucial difference between radio and television is the significance of words. Television writers use pictures to do the job of words, radio-writers use words to do the job of pictures – words designed to be lifted off the page and spoken aloud. If you listen to people talking to each other in a bus or a train you will notice that their use of language is somewhat casual and untidy. In ordinary conversation people pause, stumble, and pick themselves up. They speak in short phrases and incomplete sentences as the thoughts come into their minds. They repeat words although the sense does not require it; they do not try to find different words to avoid overworking the same ones; and even educated people can be very ungrammatical in conversation.

Consider two reports of the same event, first as you might read it in a local newspaper:

TEENAGER FEARED KIDNAPPED

Police fear that pretty dark-haired Mary Smith who failed to return from shopping on Saturday afternoon may have been kidnapped. Wearing a fluorescent red anorak and jeans she was last seen by school-friend Joan Brown in Ambridge High Street at 3.15 pm. Joan says 'She was going to buy a skirt and then go home. She's not the sort of girl to do anything silly. I hope nothing has happened to her!' Police enquiries are continuing.

Now listen to Joan Brown talking to a friend on the telephone:

Hallo! Betty! Can you hear me? This is a dreadful line. Listen – an awful thing has happened. You know Mary Smith? The dark girl with curly hair? She's disappeared – gone missing! I saw her in the High Street on Saturday afternoon. She was wearing a new anorak – said her mother had given it to her for Christmas. Bright red, it was – what do they call it? fluorescent. She was hunting for a skirt to go with it. Then she was going to get the bus home. But she never arrived! They're saying on the radio she's been kidnapped. Isn't it dreadful?

The structure of each of these reports is quite different. The newspaper report is impersonal and factual, and packs in everything possible at the beginning. The reporter has written it in such a way that the sub-editor can cut it from the end, and even if he only has room for one sentence the story is there. The sensational headline tells all, even if hurried readers merely glance at the page. But just try reading that paragraph aloud! People do not talk like that.

Now compare the telephone conversation. First, Joan makes sure her friend is listening and gives her a teaser to heighten the suspense. With her listener hooked she then tells her story in short bursts, one scrap of information at a time, building it phrase by phrase to a climax. Joan has a proper sense of drama and has, in fact, produced the microcosm of a successful radio talk. Incidentally, she has also followed the journalistic maxim 'Tell them what you're going to tell them, then tell them, then tell them you've told them.'

Skilful writing for speech, however, means more than just transcribing the normal features of everyday conversation. It is a question of combining careful structure and imaginative use of language with an effect of spontaneity.

Scripted discussion

In the early days of radio, when the authorities were afraid of letting anyone loose on the air without a script and tape-editing was unheard-of, there was a programme format called the 'scripted discussion'. Three or four speakers would be brought together with a chairman in a studio to talk about the subject of the proposed broadcast. The conversation would be recorded and then transcribed, word for word. This was called 'telediphoning', and usually it yielded an astonishingly unreadable result. The producer would sit down with the transcript and edit it into a tidy, logical well-structured script without 'ers' and 'I means' and 'you knows', in which all the desired points were properly brought out. Finally the participants would be brought to the studio again to read the scripted version of their own words, and this would be broadcast live as a 'spontaneous' discussion. The trouble with this technique was that the speakers were being asked to behave like actors. Many people can talk with animation on a topic they feel strongly about, but it takes skill and practice to read dialogue convincingly from a script, even if the words were your own in the first place. The scripted discussion format produced some flat and stilted results and was soon abandoned.

Scripted talks

The scripted talk, however, is still very much alive, and the technique of recording and transcribing your own words is a useful one in drafting a script you are going to deliver yourself. You will have to be prepared to do this if you are putting forward your own views or describing a personal experience. In general, broadcasting organisations do not buy talks scripts from one person to be read by another. Listeners like to feel that they are meeting, over the air, the actual person who . . . climbed the mountain, broke the speed record, objects strongly to the new law, or has personal expertise in putting new washers on taps . . . whatever the subject may be. Short stories are a different matter, but more of that later.

Listen to yourself on a tape recorder. The experience of hearing yourself recorded for the first time is usually unpleasant. Who is this stranger with the funny squeaky voice and the appalling vowels? Do you really sound like that? Your friends assure you it is exactly like you, just as they do when they show you an unflattering snapshot. It is a curious fact that the microphone seems to exaggerate individual vocal traits. You will never before have heard your voice as others hear it, because in the ordinary way it reverberates inside your head as well as coming to your ears across an air gap. But this stranger is the person your audience will meet. If you are to write successfully for yourself you must study your own style of speech, come to terms with your own vocal personality, and construct the sort of sentences that will sit easily on your tongue.

19

Don't worry if a foreign or regional accent is more marked than you had believed, provided you can be clearly understood. It is probably what gives your way of speech its special character. Time was when non-standard English would have been considered a disadvantage, but nowadays for all except would-be newsreaders and announcers a foreign or regional flavour in the voice can be a distinct asset. Think of the many top broadcasters with an Irish brogue! Thick dialect can be hard to understand for those unfamiliar with it, and this has to be watched, but the odd dialect word or expression can bring vitality to an otherwise bland script.

One of the most successful practitioners of the broadcast talk was the writer J. B. Priestley. He had a warm, friendly vocal personality, with a strong flavour of his native Yorkshire, and the seven-minute 'Postscripts' that he broadcast on Sunday evenings after the Nine o'clock news during the first summer of the war in 1940 are classics of the medium. They drew such a response from listeners that they were published in book form, with a preface by Priestley himself. He points out that they were 'meant to be spoken and heard over the air and not to be read in cold print . . . wireless talks and not essays.' Two important conclusions emerged, he said, from his experience of broadcasting these Postscripts:

> The first, and less important, is the immense, the staggering power and effect of broadcasting . . . as a medium of communication broadcasting makes everything else seem like the method of a secret society. So long as you don't go on too long and the listeners are not tired of you, a mere whisper over the air seems to start an avalanche. Mention a couple of ducks and they are photographed as if they were film stars. Refer to a pie in a shop window, and instantly there are pilgrimages to it . . .
>
> The second and more important conclusion that emerges from this short chapter of broadcasting experience is that . . . what holds the attention of most decent folk is a genuine sharing of feelings and views on the part of the broadcaster. He must talk as if he were among serious friends, and not as if he had suddenly been appointed head of an infants' school. People may be almost inarticulate themselves, and yet recognise in an instant when something that is at least trying to be real and true is being said to them.

If you are to be a successful broadcaster you must learn to read your own words as if they had just come into your mind. So use the tape recorder as a means of drafting your talk. Write out exactly what you said, and then edit and re-organise it. Resist the temptation to condense the sentences and tidy them up. Leave in the repetitions and the short uneven phrases. Consider the punctuation: punctuation for speech is different from punctuation for print. In speech it is used more like the dynamic signs in music. You will need more commas to mark the phrases, and a liberal use of dashes can be helpful.

Your talk will be intended for a particular broadcasting slot, so you will write with a specific length in mind. A page of A4 typescript in double spacing will take about two minutes to read aloud – roughly 140 words a minute, depending on the sort of material and the way you talk. Work with a stopwatch, and tailor your script carefully for length. If your draft is too long, prune it by taking out whole sentences or paragraphs rather than condensing it by means of subordinate clauses. Do not be tempted into believing that you can shorten it by speaking faster. Remember, also, that when you are reading aloud to an actual audience you will automatically read more slowly than when you are reading only to yourself.

Identify the boring words and look for vivid expressions to substitute for them – words that will conjure up pictures in your listeners' minds. Remember you need to make them hear, smell, and feel as well as see. Keep the personal sense of involvement always alive before them. Not 'Egypt is hot in July', but 'I was sweating in the humid Egyptian summer'. Brian Hanrahan gave a classic demonstration of this in a famous despatch during the Falklands War. He was describing an air strike from a British carrier, and was not allowed to give details of the forces involved. Instead of saying 'Our aircraft suffered no losses', he said 'I counted them all out and I counted them all back' – and in imagination his listeners stood on the deck with him.

If you need to put over facts and figures which may be difficult for a listener to grasp, try to put the information in an easily understandable way. For example, instead of giving measurements and figures use a simile such as 'the size of a tennis court' or 'enough people to fill Wembley Stadium.' If it is essential for precise details to be conveyed, for example the quantities in a cookery recipe, suggest at the start that your listeners have pencil and paper handy so that you can repeat the ingredients slowly at the end of your talk, or give an address where people can write for a handout.

A word of warning about humour and irony: Remember that your audience cannot see your facial expression. 'A smile in the voice' is something skilled broadcasters know how to achieve, but it takes practice, and in its absence listeners may easily misunderstand the spirit of some dryly witty comment.

When you have made your script as effective as you know how, type it out, in double-spacing on one side of the paper only, and send it with a short covering letter to the producer of the programme to which you want to contribute. You can, if you like, send a cassette as well, to give the producer an idea of your vocal personality. This cassette will almost certainly not be broadcast. Instead, if your script is liked, you will be invited to go to the studio and record it, or perhaps broadcast it 'live'. More guidance on submitting scripts and ideas is given in Chapter 12 on Markets, Fees and Copyright.

Short stories

It may be that you want to write short stories for radio, and in this case, your script will probably be given to someone else to read – unless, that is, you are a professional actor yourself. The standard BBC slot for short stories is fifteen minutes long, which means about 2,300 words. The important thing here is to create characters that an actor can bring to life in his performance. First person stories, in which the tale is told by a clearly characterised narrator, are often particularly successful, and it is wise in any case to confine yourself to one person's viewpoint. It may help to think of a short story as a play for one voice.

The opening of a short story is crucial. Within the first few moments the audience has to 'tune in' to the voice and character of the narrator, and decide whether or not to go on listening. It is important, however, not to give a piece of information that is vital to the enjoyment of the rest of the story in the very first sentence. People switch on late, and often for a variety of reasons fail to register the first few words. Arouse the listener's curiosity with an intriguing opening, offer him believable characters which can be brought to life by a skilled reader, and round your story off with a satisfying end. Although many short stories have a twist in the tail this is by no means essential, so long as the end feels 'right' to the listener. The BBC's main short story slot at present is on Radio 4 at 4.45 in the afternoon. Local radio stations sometimes broadcast them in the middle of the night, for the benefit of shift workers and insomniacs. The mood of an audience changes subtly over the 24 hours, and broadcasters learn how to take this into account in scheduling and manner of presentation.

Continuity and presentation

Each network has its own individual style, and it is quite possible to tell from the sound of a channel, before you have distinguished a single word or heard a station ident, which one you are listening to. Brash, brisk Radio 1 contrasts sharply with the more easy-going approach of Radio 2, while the scholarly announcements which sometimes preface programmes on Radio 3 are quite different from the straightforward, journalistic presentation on Radio 4 or Radio 5 Live. Local radio stations also each have their own 'house style', on which they have built their listening figures. Writing continuity and announcements for each station calls for a different approach, in tune with the expectations of the audience. We come back to one of the key points made at the beginning of this book: empathy with the audience is a key ingredient in successful broadcasting.

4. Using Actuality; Tape-recording and Editing

Broadcasting was transformed by the invention of the portable tape recorder. Until the late 1940s the standard method of recording was on big slow-speed acetate discs. The heavy twin-tabled recording gear was mounted in large saloon cars from which the microphones would be run out on long cables. This cumbersome paraphernalia put severe limitations on where recordings could be made. It also meant that a recording team with its driver and engineer was nearly the size of a film crew, and recording sessions had to be planned carefully in advance.

Editing with slow-speed discs was a complex business. One of the best-known programmes to be recorded on location was Wilfred Pickles' quiz show, *Have a Go*. This took up several discs and did not always run to time, so a certain amount of cutting had to be done to fit the programme to its slot. The discs were recorded with an overlap, and on transmission the operator would start the two discs and get them running side by side in sync. for a few moments before mixing over from one to the next. It was possible sometimes to shorten the recording by lifting the needle early on disc one, or dropping it late on disc 2. But Wilfred sometimes got carried away by his live audience, and either the backchat and repartee would become indiscreet or some competitor would mention a brand name or make a libellous statement which could not be broadcast. This would somehow have to be removed from the middle of a disc. If time permitted this could be done by 'dubbing off' (copying), however the programme was often recorded only hours before transmission, so time was at a premium and the editing had to be done by 'jump cuts'. The discs would be marked up with chinagraph pencil, and as the operator played them on the air he would listen with a cue sheet, lift the needle at the critical point, and drop it again *on the right groove* a few seconds further on. This called for nerve and skill, and I have often seen the operator emerge from the Manchester studio limp with exhaustion after a gruelling session of playing *Have a Go* with more than its usual quota of jump-cuts.

The advent of magnetic tape changed all this. Programmes could now be recorded and replayed continuously, whatever the duration, and any necessary cuts could easily be made with a razor-blade and a reel of splicing tape.

It took time to develop a truly portable recorder. The heavy and cumbersome 'Midget' recorder was scarcely worthy of the name, but it released the broadcaster from the umbilical cord of the recording car. He became free to make recordings wherever and whenever he chose, and the age of unscripted actuality was born.

Now that the tyranny of the script and the formal recording session had been broken the way was clear for a whole fresh class of broadcaster to take to the air. Men and women who fluffed and stumbled, who spoke in thick dialect and found it impossible to read fluently from a script, were 'discovered' as a new and exciting source of broadcast material. Even tapes recorded by someone with a pronounced stutter could be cleaned up to produce a smooth and apparently spontaneous result. There were times when the whole personality of a speaker was removed by over-enthusiastic editing, but the tape recorder was a big bonus for the radio producer.

The birth of the radio ballad

One man who saw the imaginative and creative possibilities in this new technology was Charles Parker, a BBC Producer in Birmingham. He started to collect recordings of men and women talking about their work and experiences of life, and was struck by the natural vitality of this sort of talk, and how impossible it was ever to recreate it in the studio with actors. He had the idea of telling a dramatic story entirely through words spoken by the actual people to whom it had happened, using no narrator, but only the authentic voices edited into a montage and heightened by music. He chose as collaborators the poet and folk-singer Ewan McColl and the musician Peggy Seeger, and the result was a new art form – the Radio Ballad.

The first Radio Ballad told the story of John Axon, the driver of a runaway goods train who stayed on his footplate when he could have jumped to safety. He failed to regain control of his engine and was killed when he crashed into a train in front. *The Ballad of John Axon* was first broadcast in 1958, and was a sensation. John Axon was followed by a programme about the North Sea fishermen, *Singing the Fishing*, which won the Italia Prize. Here is how Charles Parker himself described the process of creating a Radio Ballad:

> You go out and talk for hours and hours and hours with the people who are the subject, not interviewing them, just listening to them, so that you begin to get under your belt as a writer, as a producer, as a singer, what it's like to be a fisherman, or to be a fisherman's wife, and to live in a fishing community; and you record also all the sounds that surround this activity as part of the scene in which this life takes place, and you come away – as we came away in this case – with something like fifty or sixty hours of material. You then transcribe that, and from those transcriptions you write songs, and you begin to see a pattern for a programme called, in this case, *Singing the Fishing*. It's called 'THE fishing', and that very simple use of the definite article carries a tremendous weight. Like 'Fisher' – when you say 'I'm fisher' that means 'fisher-folk', and much stronger than 'fisher-folk' it carries all sorts of undertones of struggle and hardship and privation and pride. That's what you learn when you listen.

Ewan McColl, Charles Parker's folk-singer/collaborator, had this advice for young people going into radio or television:

> I would say the first thing is to learn how to listen. And fortunately one has a machine which is a constant guide and a constant friend in helping one to learn how to listen and that machine is the tape recorder. I would say, go out, as we did . . . with a tape recorder and start off with the premise that you know nothing, but that out there in the big world outside there are people who know everything if you're prepared to listen. And if one is humble enough to . . . engage a bus driver or a waitress, or a building worker or whatever for as long as they're prepared to talk then you will get something absolutely fantastic. At first people will tell you the things they think you want to hear, then they'll talk off the top of their heads. But there will come a time when they get

tired of doing that and what will come out is something very very important and very very beautiful . . .

Listening to *The Ballad of John Axon*, or to *Singing the Fishing* is a riveting experience. At the time of writing recordings are still available in libraries, and once in a while they are given the accolade of repeat broadcasts. Charles Parker died sadly young, but his work was a landmark in the recognition of the poetic value of vernacular speech. It is good to know that his tapes and materials have been collected together under the auspices of the Charles Parker Foundation, set up by his friends at Birmingham University. Among dedicated radio-writers his name will not be forgotten.

Recording now: audio-tape

Today every other person owns a cassette tape recorder, often small and light enough to carry in a pocket. For the professional broadcaster, however, an open-reel machine has until recently been essential. With the arrival of digital recording technology, audio-tape will soon be superseded. It will probably be a year or two before tape-recorders become entirely obsolete, so the next part of this chapter deals with the time-honoured techniques of making and editing recordings on ¼ inch audio-tape.

Audio tape runs at four standard speeds: 15, 7½, 3½ and 1⅞ inches per second. The higher the tape speed the better the quality of recording and reproduction. Broadcasting companies have tended to use 15 ips for music, in order to accommodate the full frequency range required. 7½ ips produces acceptable quality for speech, and tapes recorded at this speed are easy to edit. It is possible, though more difficult, to razor-edit 3¾ ips tapes, but with the narrower cassette tapes recorded at 1⅞ ips the only option is to edit electronically by dubbing (copying). If you have valuable material on a cassette tape, however, it is possible to copy it up onto ¼ inch open reel tape at a higher speed and edit it in that form.

It is never satisfactory to rely on the integral microphone supplied with many cassette-recorders, except for the most basic purposes – for example to tape the speeches at a meeting for subsequent transcription. Money spent on the best possible microphone is always an investment, and it should be fitted with a sufficient length of cable to enable you to set it up well away from the actual recording machine, in order to avoid picking up motor noise.

If you plan to do a lot of broadcasting you will need a stop-watch as well. Make sure you buy the type that will accumulate – i.e. one that you will be able to stop and restart without resetting. You can then time the cuts in a talk or recording as you make them, without constantly having to re-time the whole thing from the beginning.

Most modern tape recorders are half-track, i.e. you can make a first recording with the tape running one way and then turn the reel over and make a second recording on the other half of the tape, running in the reverse direction. Don't be tempted to do this if there is any likelihood that you will ever wish to edit the tape. It is a false economy. As soon as you cut one track you will also cut the other and ruin your second recording.

For many years the standard tool of the radio reporter has been the UHER, which runs either on mains electricity or rechargeable batteries. This piece of professional equipment is expensive but essential. Some radio stations will lend UHERs to freelance contributors who know how to use them. New portable battery/mains tape recorders may come onto the market, but whatever the machine you record with, although it may improve the technical quality of your recording, it will not alter the value of what you put on the tape.

Editing audio-tape

The technique of razor-editing is simple. You need:

- a white or yellow chinagraph pencil
- a one-sided razor-blade or surgical scalpel
- a reel of special splicing tape
- reels of coloured leader tape – red, green and white.
- an EMI editing block

The EMI editing block is a solid block of metal measuring about 6 inches long by 1 inch wide by ½ inch deep, with a quarter inch channel down the middle, intersected by three narrow grooves running at 90, 45 and 33 degrees to the central channel. I have only ever used the 90 degree groove. Do not be tempted into buying smaller light-weight blocks, or gadgets with springs and grips for holding the tape – they are more trouble than they are worth.

The technique is as follows:

1) Mark the tape with the chinagraph pencil either side of the desired cut. In order to do this it is often necessary to unscrew the cover of the tape recorder to gain access to the replay head. Put the machine into *play* mode and activate the *pause* control. You should then be able to rotate the tape-reels by hand very slowly so as to identify the exact point at which a word or a cough begins or ends. This is called 'rock and roll' editing.

2) Lay the tape in the central channel so that the first mark falls on the 45 degree cross-groove, and cut it with the scalpel. Leave the end of tape you want to keep lying in the channel.

3) Bring up the other end of the tape, lay the mark on the groove, and cut it with the scalpel. You can now lift away the excised section of tape, leaving the two bits you want to keep held end-to-end in the central channel. (Don't throw away the discarded section yet).

4) Cut a half-inch bit of splicing tape and lay it over the join, pressing it well down to make sure it sticks.

5) Remove your edited tape from the block and check the edit by running it through the tape-recorder and listening to it critically.

You may change your mind about the way you have cut the tape, and it is perfectly possible to stick a section of excised tape back and re-edit at a different point, *provided you have kept the bit you cut and remember which way the tape runs*. I have always found it a useful practice to hang the surplus tape round my neck until I have checked the edit.

Put a length of green leader-tape at the start of your edited tape, and a length of red at the end. Intermediate sections can, if you like, be marked with white leader. Make sure your leaders are long enough to go round the tape decks of the large professional machines in a broadcasting studio.

Editing is time-consuming and tedious, but the more practice you have the faster you can get. It is valuable to be able to do it on your own at home instead of having to book expensive studio sessions.

Although it is legitimate to remove long pauses in a recording of a hesitant speaker, it is important to retain the natural gaps between words and phrases. For this reason, when marking the tape, make the first mark at the start of the first word to be cut, and the second mark at the start of the first word to be heard after the cut, thus retaining the natural pacing of the sentence. For example:

> . . . sounds that surround this activity as part of the – /part of the sort of – /scene in which this life takes place

Not

> . . . sounds that surround this activity as part of the/ – part of the sort of – /scene in which this life takes place

In the hands of an unscrupulous editor a tape can be made to suggest that a speaker said things he did not say. Negatives can be removed, words transposed, whole sentences built up from different sections of the original tape, and when replayed the cuts will be undetectable. In the hands of a Goebbels audio tape could be a devastating weapon of propaganda. In Britain we may hope that traditions of integrity in radio journalism ensure that tape editing is used with discretion to enhance the acceptability of a speaker and not to distort his views.

Recording conditions

The quality of recorded sound is affected by the surroundings in which the recording is made. Large echoing rooms with hard shiny surfaces such as polished floors and plate glass windows tend to give unsatisfactory results. Try to find a small room or the corner of a corridor. Draw curtains across windows, put a blanket or coat under the microphone on a table to deaden reflections.

Listen for intrusive external noises such as lawn mowers or vacuum cleaners, and try to get them halted while you are recording. If an aircraft flies overhead, stop your recording and restart after it has passed. Not only will irrelevant sounds be a distraction, they will make it difficult for you to edit the tape. If Concorde flying overhead suddenly stops dead because you cut out the next sentence your listeners will wonder what has happened.

Music in the background adds another hazard – that of copyright. If you are not able to provide full details of composer, performers and recording label of any music heard on your tape it may be impossible to clear copyright, and consequently impossible to broadcast it. A cautionary example is the song 'Happy birthday to you'. This is in copyright, and a fee is payable every time it is broadcast.

There is no doubt that the skilful inclusion of appropriate background sounds can create an atmosphere of authenticity in a broadcast, and give the listener a sense of actually being there. It is difficult, however, to judge the balance of these against voices when you are recording. The wisest course is to make two separate recordings, one in a quiet corner carrying your interview or whatever, and one carrying the sound effects which can eventually be mixed in at the right level in the studio when the tapes are broadcast.

Before you set out to make a recording involving anyone else, make sure you are perfectly familiar with your equipment, and make a test recording before you start. Don't forget to deactivate the replay volume, otherwise you will get a 'howl-round' the minute you open the microphone. If the tape doesn't move when you switch on, this is probably because it has been incorrectly laced, or you have depressed the pause control and forgotten to release it.

Rewind your tapes, box them and label them carefully with date, contents, and speed of recording. A surprising amount of time can be wasted discovering that tapes are back to front, or don't carry the material you thought they did. Routine housekeeping is essential.

Recording: the future is digital

The portable recording machine of the future is already with us. It is small and light, and uses computer discs instead of audiotape. It is relatively inexpensive, but the cost rises dramatically when editing comes into the story. This means that it is easy to acquire the means of making good audio recordings in the field (the SONY Minidisk is being widely bought by both BBC and Independent Local Radio stations) but the freelance will require access to extremely expensive editing equipment before he can re-arrange and collate his material. Gone are the happy days of scissors-and-tape and rock-and-roll editing – computer-literacy is an essential skill for the future broadcaster.

There is no consensus on the merits of the different editing formats now becoming available, and the whole recording scene is very confused. It is rather like the situation with video-tape recording in the early 1960s, when no-one quite knew which format would come out on top and scoop the market.

Ian Betson in his book *Portable Recording* has put forward the following view of likely future developments:

> In the long term, it is not known what course the development of the portable recorder will take. Will the 'ideal' machine be developed – one that combines all the best features but overcomes all the disadvantages of the recorders [*at present available*], one that suits anyone and everyone and, most importantly, one that suits all pockets? It's a brave person who predicts the future.
>
> Having said that, new types of machine are beginning to emerge, with new ways of operation and new ways for the user to operate. Vamos – a Dutch company – has recently released the Digicorder. It's a digital recorder – about the size of a UHER – that uses computer technology to record two hours of audio. Once recorded, the audio can be edited on the machine and sent down a digital telephone line using an on board adaptor. It all looks very promising until you find out the price – approximately £7000. One is also tempered in opting for computer hard disc technology by an industry maxim. 'There are only two types of hard disc – ones that have failed and ones that have yet to fail!'
>
> At least two manufacturers are toying with the idea of introducing a laptop computer with microphone inputs. This would allow a reporter away from base to record actuality, edit it, write an associated cue on the built-in word processor and send the whole lot, written cue and audio, back to base via a digital 'phone line for broadcast. This, in theory should allow the reporter to move quickly onto the next story and not waste time shuttling between base and story location –

much like a newspaper reporter works – write the story and phone/fax/modem it back to the newsroom for editing and printing. Extending this practice somewhat further into a, not altogether, hypothetical scenario, a radio reporter could work from home, rarely visiting the newsroom base. Prospects or jobs for the day could be sent by the duty editor to the reporter's home, anytime of the day or night, via fax or modem. The reporter then covers the story, edits it, transmits it and the cue or other written instructions back to base via the digital telephone line or mobile 'phone, then moves on to the next story. With the built-in communications features, the piece could even be broadcast straight into the on-air programme. Combined recorders/word processors/ communications devices such as these could radically alter the way the reporter works in the not-too-distant future.

Rest assured, portable recorders will be the next 'big thing' when it comes to technology in the professional broadcast/audio market place. Watch this space!

5. Drama on the Air

Every day of the week the BBC broadcasts a radio play in at least one of its domestic services. The World Service also has its own drama department. Many BBC plays reach wider audiences still through the sale of cassette recordings to the public. The result is that far more people listen to a radio play than could possibly attend a theatre during a run in London's West End. No wonder many famous writers have thought it worth while to write for this enormous and far-flung audience, and many writers now distinguished in other media including film and television served an initial apprenticeship in the fascinating and demanding field of radio drama. The BBC is always looking for new writers, and as part of this search it mounts regular competitions for playscripts. It is also particularly interested in receiving more scripts from women.

Although it is a good deal cheaper to produce a play on radio than on television, drama is more costly than other forms of programming, and radio networks financed by advertising find commercial pressures towards inexpensive mass-appeal pop-music/chat-show formats almost irresistible. Across the Atlantic radio plays have virtually disappeared from the air waves. Nevertheless, some Independent Local Radio stations in Britain continue to keep the drama flag flying. In 1987 the IBA entered a play from Radio Clyde for the prestigious international Italia Prize contest, and an adaptation of *Pepys' Diary*, made by Independent Radio Drama Productions Ltd in a series of ten five-minute instalments was broadcast successfully by LBC. Competitions for original radio plays have been sponsored by, among others, Marks and Spencer in association with the Highland Regional Council and Moray Firth Radio, and other Local Radio stations have transmitted plays written by listeners in their reception area, or productions made by local schoolchildren in association with educational producers.

Dramatic structure

What makes a good radio play? To answer that question we must first consider what makes a good play in any medium, and then look at factors which lend themselves especially to radio presentation. The classic elements without which effective drama cannot exist are: an initial conflict, mounting tension, a climax, and a resolution.

Plays are made up of a sequence of scenes, which can be considered as the foothills of a mountain. As the foothills rise and fall, each one getting higher than the last until the summit is reached, so should each scene be a microcosm of the whole, with its own internal tension, climax and resolution. Although the first draft of a play, dashed off in the white heat of inspiration, may not conform to these requirements, careful editing with this structure in mind will undoubtedly heighten its dramatic effect.

Theme and plot

As well as this basic structure, our play will have a plot, characters and a theme. The plot is the sequence of events which take place in the action, the characters are the people to whom they happen, and the theme underlying the whole thing is what the play is really about. Let us suppose our play does in fact tell the story of a man climbing a mountain. The plot is constructed so as to give him various difficulties and hazards to overcome, and brings him into contact with other characters who interact with him. But the same story can be used to illustrate a number of different themes – the struggle of man against nature, self-discovery through confrontation with danger, the indomitability of the human spirit, the nature of ambition, and so on. The theme is the true raison d'être of the play, an internal pulse which beats like a heart throughout the action and gives it significance.

Pros and cons of the medium

Now let us consider the limitations imposed by the medium of radio, and the freedoms which it bestows. First, and most obvious, the audience cannot see.

Richard Hughes, the writer of the very first radio play, *Danger*, broadcast in 1924, turned this to good account by placing his characters in the same position as his audience – he set his story in a coal mine. The first words are 'What's happened?' 'The lights have gone out.' Immediately listeners can identify with the small group caught in the nightmare of a pit accident, underground in the dark.

The writer cannot call on the resources of scenery, lighting and costume to reinforce his message. The silent visual coup de théatre is denied him. But the other side of this coin is pure gold – he doesn't have to give the audience anything to look at, and this means nothing less than total freedom in time and space. This is the theatre of the mind, and the writer can move his characters instantly backwards through the centuries or forwards into the future. He can set the first scene on an airliner and the next at the bottom of the sea. If he chooses to send his protagonist to the South Pole we can go with him every step of the way. This is liberation indeed.

What is more, although the characters in a radio play must use human language they don't have to be human beings. Animals, plants and inanimate objects can be brought to articulate life and pressed into service as part of the cast. Radio lends itself particularly well to fantasy, witness the much-loved *Toy-town* and *Wind in the Willows*, and Douglas Adams' cult success of the 1980s *The Hitch-hiker's Guide to the Galaxy*.

This aspect of radio was brilliantly exploited by J.C.W. Brook in his play *Giving Up*. The plot is about one man's efforts to give up smoking. The cast list features all the parts of the body, including ears, nose, mouth, arms, legs, fingers, private parts, brain, will, conscience, and so on. This is how the play opens:

SLEEP NOISES FROM ALL OVER THE BODY

RIGHT EAR: Right ear to Brain, Right ear to Brain . . .
LEFT EAR: (OVERLAPS) Left ear to Brain, left ear to
             Brain . . .

RIGHT EAR: You keep out of this. I heard it first.
LEFT EAR: I'm only doing my job. When I hear something I
report it. Left Ear to Brain, Left Ear to Brain . . .
RIGHT EAR: (OVERLAPS) Right ear to Brain, Right Ear to
Brain . . .

GRUNTS AND GROANS AND BESTIRRING NOISES
FROM ALL OVER THE BODY.

OMNES: Shut up Ears . . . Go back to sleep . . . Stuff some
cotton wool in your orifices . . . etc.
BRAIN: (WAKES) Errrmmmmm . . . ahhh . . .ummm?
EARS: Alarm Clock, Brain – alarm clock; time to get up.

RINGING OF ALARM CLOCK COMES ECHOING
THROUGH EARS.

BRAIN: Oh dear . . .
RIGHT ARM: Right Arm here, Brain. The usual?
BRAIN: Ummm, please.
RIGHT ARM: Stretching now . . . (STRETCHING NOISES)
O.K. Fingers, first one on the button gets a
manicure.

Giving Up J.C.W. Brook (BBC Playscripts)

And so the play continues with dialogue between all the
different elements that make up a man, and increasing conflict
between his Brain, his Will, and his Conscience. It's extremely
ingenious, highly effective radio, and would be hard to realise
in any other medium. More recently, a late night thriller
Terminus has allowed the voice of the railway station itself to
play a part in the action.

It would be a mistake to believe that dramatic writing is
necessarily confined to formal plays. Many radio commercials
are in effect one minute mini-dramas, and dramatised sequences
turn up in all sorts of unexpected places. Take the following
example in a script by Dylan Winter broadcast in *The Food
Programme* – the narrator is having a conversation with his
'fridge:

NARRATOR: Okay, What else is there to eat?
YOGGI POT CHORUS: Eat us we are the Yoggi Pots,
Yoggi Pots, Yoggi pots

	We are the Yoggi pots And we taste yum yum.
FRIDGE:	So tasteless some of the labels on the cheaper foods. I think it's getting worse, sir, than it was in our day.
FISH FINGERS:	What about us fish fingers – we've been in here since January.
NARRATOR:	What about that piece of Camembert then?
FRIDGE:	A little bit too ripe now sir for eating fresh.
CAMEMBERT:	Oh no I'm not, I'm at my very best. You'll not find a better piece of cheese in the whole of La Belle France.
FRIDGE:	Please don't bother with all that authentic Frenchness – even Mr Winter knows you come from Cornwall.
CAMEMBERT:	Devon actually me dear.
NARRATOR:	Stop bickering in there, and Fridge don't patronise me. What sort of ice-cream have you got available? I fancy indulging myself.
FRIDGE:	13 stone 6 lb.
NARRATOR:	Sorry?
FRIDGE:	13 stone 6 lb. is what you currently weigh sir, that is, I believe, more than 20 lbs over your target weight.
NARRATOR:	Crackers and Marmite again then.
FRIDGE:	Very wise decision if I may say so sir.

Dialogue and characterisation

Now for the nitty-gritty of a radio play – the dialogue. In radio the dialogue has to do much more than in any other dramatic medium. It has to carry the plot forward, portray the characters, place them in time and space, provide the props and paint the scenery. In these multifarious tasks it can be supported by music and effects, but music and effects cannot relieve the dialogue of its responsibilities – they can only assist it.

Each character should have an aurally recognisable personality. Some of this can be achieved in production by clever casting, but the groundwork must be laid by the playwright. A scene which calls for an argument between four middle-class middle-aged women will have to be skilfully acted indeed for the listener to be able to tell who is saying what. By creating scenes in which, to take crude examples, man talks to woman, foreigner to Englishman, child to adult, and not allowing too many people to join in at once, the writer automatically makes it easier for the listener to keep his bearings and differentiate between the characters.

Make sure that the characters talk consistently all the way through. A useful exercise is to read aloud all the lines given to one character, end to end in sequence throughout a play, leaving out the speeches in between. This will often throw up lines which are patently out of character, and places where character-isation can be strengthened.

Although, as we have seen, radio is an intimate medium, it is not enough for dialogue to mimic the diffuse exchanges of normal conversation. Dramatically effective dialogue is every-day speech boiled-down into a concentrated essence, in which every word has a reason for being there, whether to illustrate character, to carry the plot forward, or to build atmosphere and a sense of location. Do not overlook the potential of monologue. Shakespeare's soliloquies take on new power and significance when we hear them spoken softly as if we are in truth eaves-dropping on Hamlet's thoughts, rather than having them belted out across the footlights in order to reach the farthest corner of the gallery. There have been highly successful radio plays for one voice only.

Strong language

A word about strong language. There are many members of the radio audience who are deeply offended by swearing, blasphemy and the use of four-letter Anglo-Saxon words for functions of the body. This makes it difficult for the writer to provide convincing dialogue for characters whose everyday speech draws freely on such resources. A glance at Bob Geldof's autobiography will illustrate this amply. The fact remains that strong language is unacceptable as normal currency on the air. It is perfectly possible to create scenes of obscenity and sexual violence without using a single offensive word, and it is a test of writing skill to do this. In the end, the frequent use of bad language only weakens its effect.

The deliberate choice of a single shocking word at a climactic point may be dramatically essential. The classic example is Bernard Shaw in *Pygmalion*, when he makes Eliza Doolittle ejaculate 'Not bloody likely' in the middle of a polite tea-party. She would have to use a stronger word than 'bloody' to produce a comparable effect today, but the principle is the same.

Dialect

Characters who speak in dialect can be useful as a contrast to other voices (provided the whole play is not in dialect!), but beware of spelling out the lines given to such characters phonetically. The writer should make use of the idioms and turns of phrase natural to the dialect in question, and indicate in the list of characters that this person is a Scot or a Geordie, or whatever. The Producer will cast a player who is good at this particular accent, and the actor will do the rest. Actors find phonetic spelling at best irritating, and at worst a real hindrance to interpretation. They also prefer not to have words underlined to indicate stress. Sentences should be written so that the intended meaning is clear without underscoring particular words. Different interpretations can develop and emphases can change in a remarkable way in the course of rehearsal.

Moving characters in time and space

Now to locating the action. In a radio play there is no printed programme in which you can brief the audience 'Scene 1, Bert's living room . . . Scene 2, next morning at the boat house' etc. The locations and the passage of time must be indicated through the dialogue. A useful convention has grown up in the use of fades. A fade-out followed by a fade-up is clearly understood by the audience to signal a lapse of time and/or a change of location. These developments must, however, be 'signposted' in the dialogue.

BERT: Right, then, I'll meet you at the boat house tomorrow morning. 6.30, and don't oversleep, you old slug-a-bed.

40

TOM: (MOVING OFF) I'll be there, never fear.
BERT: (CALLING AFTER HIM) Make sure you are, then!
  (FADE)

FADE UP OPEN AIR ACOUSTIC. NOISE OF LAPPING
WATER.

BERT: Ah! Tom! You made it! Wonders will never cease.
TOM: (APPROACHING, YAWNING) I don't deny it was an
  effort. I say, the river's high this morning . . .

Note that we did not have to hear a door open and shut at the
end of the first scene as Tom left, and we certainly don't need
footsteps. Footsteps are hardly ever necessary, and when they
are required to make a special impact (for example, echoing in
a passageway as the villain stalks the heroine at dead of night
in a thriller) it is often difficult to make them sound convincing.
They have to be made on the correct surface, in the right
perspective with the actors' voices, and they need literally to be
acted out in the studio. Although recorded footsteps may be
available they seldom ring true, and an immense amount of
rehearsal time can be taken up getting footsteps just right.
Don't call for them in your script unless they are absolutely
essential.

Effects, perspective and acoustic

Sound effects (often written FX in a script) should be used with
discretion to create atmosphere rather than as a primary vehicle
of information. The best effects are clear precise noises which
are easily recognizable. The much-maligned BBC seagull is a
good example. A ship's hooter, a cuckoo, the cooing of doves,
the call of an owl, a grandfather clock striking – all these
convey instant atmosphere. Mushy sounds such as traffic, rain
and crackling fires are not immediately identifiable for what
they are, and are much less effective.

A surprising amount of information can be conveyed by the
use of perspective and acoustic. Entrances and exits are
achieved by getting a character to approach or move away from
the microphone, and good radio actors are very skilled in this
technique. Voices in a small room sound quite different from

voices in the echoing spaces of a cathedral or in the deadness of the open air, and the listener is sensitive to these distinctions. Drama studios are equipped to provide a range of acoustics. Through the control panel different degrees of artificial echo can be added to make variations between one scene and the next, and there may well be an 'an-echoic' chamber where actors can play scenes set out of doors. For this reason you should include in your script clear indications of the location of each scene, even though you don't need to give a visual description.

Stereophonic recording makes it possible to give highly realistic aural pictures of the action in a play, in which characters can be heard moving about almost as if they were on stage in a theatre. To get the full stereo effect, however, the listener must place himself accurately in relation to the loudspeakers or else listen on headphones. Most of the audience will not be doing this, and reception on the average domestic receiver falls far short of the exacting standards in a broadcasting studio. The writer must therefore not depend on skilful stereo reproduction to convey information. The play must 'work' and be fully understandable at a much less sophisticated technical level.

The listener remains with the microphone, wherever you decide to put it, and to take the microphone for a walk with two characters while they talk to each other is seldom effective. There will be no sense of movement, even if (perish the thought!) you add footsteps. It will be better to start your two characters off on their walk by losing them as they move into the distance, and then leap-frog the microphone ahead of them, so that you hear them approaching. You can do this several times, and it works well. Note that there is a difference between a move off and a fade out. The first indicates a simple exit, while the second suggests a lapse of time as well.

Some years ago the Actor-Manager Timothy West wrote a short play called *This Gun I have in my Right Hand is Loaded*. This hilarious piece neatly sends up the conventions of radio drama. The fact is that although the conventions work they have to be used with subtlety and discretion. I am grateful to Mr West for permission to include his masterpiece at the end of this book, as a cautionary example for aspiring radio playwrights.

Music

Music is a powerful generator of atmosphere and mood, and can be introduced in several ways. Perhaps one of the characters is a musician, and the music he plays is an integral part of the action. Or perhaps a particular passage is used to signal, say, the appearance of a ghost, or the revival of a memory. Or the music may simply give the listener a clue as to the sort of story he is going to be offered, romantic or humorous, light-hearted or grim.

The selection of music is part of the Producer's job, but the writer can make suggestions if he wishes. It is often difficult to find passages of the right length and scale in standard musical works, and electronic music may be the most appropriate choice. In the early 1950s a small group of studio engineers and music balancers at the BBC began to experiment with the manufacture of all sorts of unusual sounds, musical and otherwise, and their efforts led to the establishment of the BBC Radiophonic Workshop. This is a department which employs composers and electronic engineers, and Radio and TV Producers can commission it to supply suitable music and effects for radio or television productions of all sorts, ranging from comedy shows such as the *Goons* or *Week-ending*, through a whole gamut of signature tunes for regular programmes, to prestige wild-life spectaculars.

A spin-off from this development is that the BBC now possesses an extensive library of specially composed electronic music and sounds on which it can draw for current productions, without incurring the copyright fees inevitably attracted by the use of commercial recordings.

Titles and synopses

Let us suppose that an idea for a radio play has hatched in your fertile mind. You have been mulling over the plot and its underlying theme for some time, and now you can hear the characters beginning to talk. Think of a title, even if it is only a temporary or 'working' title. This often helps to clarify the theme. Write a synopsis, a bare outline of the plot, on a single page. Draw up a list of the main characters and give them names. Don't call them 'Voice 1' and 'Voice 2' etc. There is a need for a lot more information about them than will actually be given in the script. Your play will take place at a climactic point in their lives, and you need to know them so thoroughly that you can imagine how they will behave and talk under any circumstances. The situations in which you place them will create the drama.

As you proceed with the actual writing you will find yourself referring back to the synopsis and character sketches that you prepared to start with. You may want to modify them as the play takes on a life of its own, but your original notes will help you to be consistent, and to produce something with a strong basic structure.

The BBC Radio Department produces a leaflet called 'Writing Plays for Radio' which will show you, among other things, how to set the script out on the page. The most important thing is to make a clear distinction between words meant to be spoken as dialogue and instructions as to sound effects and stage directions. Allow wide margins, double-spacing between each speech, and use only one side of the paper.

The BBC also produces another leaflet, 'Notes for Writers and Commissioning of Drama on BBC Radio', which contains information about the slots for which plays are currently being sought.

The right ending

Bear in mind that a play should be conceived not merely as a tale that is told; this is the province of the short story or the novel. A play should be an experience shared between the characters and the audience. Listeners must live through the events portrayed and participate in the emotions and motivations of those to whom they happen. They must be able to identify themselves with at least one of these characters, and feel concern and involvement in the outcome of the events. At the end, they must be left with a sense of 'rightness'. Whether the conclusion is happy or sad, the audience must not feel cheated. The ending should tidy up any unfinished business left hanging in the plot and return us to the level of everyday life from the heightened tensions of dramatic experience.

Perhaps one could parallel the mental experience of listening to a good play with the physical experience of a searching work-out, ending with a short period of relaxation, and leaving behind a sensation of adjustment, balance, and wellbeing. Maybe this is what Aristotle had in mind when he wrote of 'catharsis'. Jean-Louis Barrault puts it like this:

> In fact, at the theatre, we are always assisting at a vast settling of accounts. From all the opposing rights, from the Rugby scrum of rights, there should by degrees emerge a Sentence. Justice. And the spectator isn't satisfied unless the sentence is just. Just, not in relation to the individuals participating in the conflict, but in relation to Life, in the universal sense of the word . . . Always make sure that the universal spirit of justice has been respected in a play. If not: beware of the mood of the audience.

(from *Reflections on the Theatre*, Jean-Louis Barrault (Rockliff 1951)

Keep your eye on the *Radio Times*. It is important to listen to current radio drama, to familiarise yourself with the work of different producers, and to visualise where your play might fit into the schedules.

6. Serials and Soap Operas: Writing in a Team

There is a difference between a serial play and a soap opera. A serial play is complete in itself, although it may be broken up into several instalments. It may be an original story, or the dramatisation of a novel, but it will have a beginning, a middle and an end. A soap opera, on the other hand, is a continuously unfolding saga about a group of characters and their daily lives. It may go on for years, and when it starts no-one can foresee what the end will be – if, in fact, it ever has one. The term 'soap opera' for this form of drama is said to have originated in the USA, because it was so popular as a means of promoting the sales of soap powders. A serial play will probably be scripted by one writer, while a soap opera will involve a team. Famous serials have included Galsworthy's *Forsyte Saga*, novels by Jane Austen and Trollope, and Tolkien's *Lord of the Rings*.

Probably the best known soap opera in the world is *The Archers*, which has been running on BBC six days a week since 1951. This 'every day story of country folk' was conceived by Godfrey Basely, at that time the BBC's farming talks producer in the Midlands. He wanted to devise a programme which farmers and their families would enjoy listening to, and at the same time absorb a certain amount of accurate information about current thinking in the agricultural world. With the years the emphasis has shifted from information to entertainment, but the programme still has an agricultural adviser and is as true to present day farming life as possible. When it was launched no-one dreamed how popular it would become. Nowadays, as well as two daily UK transmissions Monday to Friday and an omnibus edition on Sundays, *The Archers* goes to many overseas destinations. Recordings are made available to the British Forces Broadcasting Service a fortnight ahead of transmission, so that service families on foreign stations can listen to the programmes on the same day as those at home in Britain, and so keep in touch with the changing seasons and day-to-day concerns of an English village community. *The Archers* has not been the only British radio serial. We have had the adventure serial *Dick Barton, Special Agent*, the domestic *Mrs Dales Diary*, and others.

Schedules

Writing scripts for a soap opera means contributing to a tightly co-ordinated operation. Getting a daily instalment on the air calls for a production-line approach which is somewhat different from the way in which many creative writers like to work. Scripts must be the right length, well-plotted and researched, skilfully characterised, written within a specified time-span, and delivered to a deadline. A late script, or one that needs rewriting, will hold up the whole conveyor-belt. It is not practical to keep a daily serial on the air with only one writer, although this can be done for short periods. The normal practice is to have a team of writers, who are given a week's episodes at a time to write. *The Archers* is run on a four-week cycle, and the following dates from the spring of 1994 are given as an example:

Mon. May 16th: All-day script meeting with eight writers, Editor, Senior Producer, Producer, Programme Assistant, Agricultural Adviser and occasionally others. The programme has a number of advisers – medical, church, land agency and so-on – and they may be at the script meeting. Four weeks' scripts are discussed and main plot-lines agreed.

Wed. May 18th: Full story-lines for four weeks sent out to four writers who are writing this month (and copies for info to all other writers).

Tues. May 24th: Four writers submit full synopsis of their week's episodes with casting details.

Wed.–Fri. May 25th–27th: Editor responds by telephone to writers synopsis and office is confirming all casting with writers.

Mon. May 30th–Sat. June 4th: Six days in studio in which previous months' scripts are recorded for transmission one month later.

Tues. June 7th: Scripts delivered.

Wed.–Thurs. June 8th–9th: Scripts edited and any rewrites needed confirmed with writers.

Mon. June 13th: Rewrites delivered by writers. Next script meeting.

In the gap between script meeting and recording all sorts of things may go wrong. A plot line one writer wants to emphasise may not have been set up sufficiently by the preceding writer. An actor may have taken work elsewhere and become unavailable for recording. Another actor playing a key character may be taken ill, and an episode have to be rewritten. Some event may occur in the real world which cannot be ignored in a programme with any pretensions to topicality. This sort of emergency can be handled provided the system works, and any unnecessary crises are avoided. Getting efficient scripts in on time is a key element of the system.

Plotting

Writers receive copies of all the latest story-lines and are asked how they think these plots should be developed. They are also asked to come up with new ideas of their own. They should bring all this to the script meeting and take part in the discussion, which is the most creative part of the 'soap-making' process. The story-lines grow out of the discussion, and writers pool their ideas at the script meeting. They sometimes have to accept that someone else is going to be given the chance to write their bright invention – all part of the angst of being a team member.

If you become part of this operation you will have to take account of the story up to the point at which you take over, and what you write will affect what everyone else writes afterwards. You will be presented with the main set of characters on whom you can draw, each of them with a fully developed life history, likes, dislikes and ways of behaviour. All sorts of things are 'known' about these people, from long before they ever appeared in the serial, and you will have to familiarise yourself with them, their backgrounds, and the geography of their surroundings. Actors are booked ad hoc, and the production office will have to make sure which of the regular performers are available before you write those characters into your script. Extra characters you may wish to bring in will be rationed. It's important to have mercy on the writer who will follow you, and not to leave him to pick up an under-developed plot line, or to extricate the characters from an impossible predicament. Think your situations right through – it isn't always practical to use the old Dick Barton get-out 'With one bound he was free!'

Structure

Each episode of *The Archers* lasts fifteen minutes, which means in practice a reading-out-loud time of about thirteen minutes. Each instalment usually contains five scenes, and not more than seven characters. The plotting is the longest and most demanding part of the process. Some writers actually do this on graph paper, ensuring that story-lines peak in the right places in the week to keep listeners tuned in. Each writer should have been given a mix of plot-lines at the meeting – something funny, something romantic, something agricultural etc. He should get a clear idea of what his main story is for the week, and his second story, and so on, otherwise the scripts can come in flat. What the Producer looks for is peaks and troughs in the right places.

Each 15 minute episode needs to be planned for a good mix. A writer should ask himself if there is a variety of tones. An echo-y barn interior might follow a breezy scene on Lakey Hill; a cosy slow-moving chat among the old folk of Ambridge might be followed by a snappy, funny scene with younger characters; an emotional scene might need a comic scene to pick the audience up again. Each scene needs to 'thicken' at its ending, and in some way signpost the listeners on: the momentum of a soap is always onwards. There might be three peaks in a week as the different story-lines come to fruition, and the last scene on a Friday needs a good strong ending. It can just be a happy ending, or a mysterious one, or a funny one, but it certainly needs to be strong.

Structuring scripts is the hardest and longest part of the process. Writers send their synopses in before casting, and the Producer and Editor hope to spot the structural errors before they go down on paper. But telling a writer one scene doesn't work can bring his whole plan for the week crumbling down around him, so writers need to be flexible. The most common problem is the balancing of action and reaction. How much should actually happen in a scene, and how much can be reported action, or characterisation, or atmosphere? A useful guideline is that at least one piece of action should happen in every scene. It may take place in the course of the dialogue (e.g. someone finds out something they didn't know before), but there should be just one piece of plot advancement. That leaves plenty of room for characterisation etc., but it means the listeners who just want plot are getting a helping in every scene.

The Archers has its own atmosphere. It reflects the tempo of life in a small rural community. If you were writing an adventure serial the pace would be much faster. There might well be three main peaks in each instalment. The first few minutes would deal with the situation obtaining at the end of the previous transmission, and build up quickly to its conclusion. The tension could then be allowed to relax as a fresh situation was introduced and developed. This in its turn would be tidied up, in time to present the third situation, which as it unfolded would generate more tension, culminating in a peak of excitement at the end of the instalment. This situation would be resolved at the start of the next day's broadcast. And so on. The most important peak – in the case of an adventure serial this would be a genuine cliff-hanger – would come at the end of the week's episodes, to hook the audience firmly into switching on again next week.

Openings

If you feel brave enough to risk your sanity on the treadmill of serial-writing, start by listening regularly, so that you absorb the atmosphere and characters of the main protagonists, and know instinctively how they would talk and react to different situations. Then write to the Producer and say you would like to try your hand. You will probably be sent a 'Writer's Pack' with all the key information, and invited to submit a trial script, either the next one after a current episode, or a completely independent one of your own devising, using main characters but ignoring current plot-lines.

Vanessa Whitburn, Editor of *The Archers*, says

Since I've been running the programme, I've established a team of eight writers who are guaranteed a number of weeks writing over the year. They come to every script meeting, even when they are not writing. This ensures a team approach and a consistent sharing and development of ideas. It does, however, make it even harder for new writers to get onto the team. However, we have a stand-by system of one or two writers in waiting. If you want to join the team you need to know that I'm looking for writers who know the programme and its history and are familiar with the characters. They need to be able to work fast, be adaptable to changing circumstances (e.g. the sudden un-availability of an actor or change in story-line) and be strong on structure. It's no good being 'precious' with ideas or slow in coming forward with them at meetings. As well as the monthly detailed script meetings we have two long-term meetings per year at which we discuss major story-line trends and map out the skeleton of our big long-running stories.

Writers need to have some knowledge of the countryside and of agriculture and a firm grip on what is dramatic. There are 'rules' that have to be obeyed concerning structure and, for example, the number of characters which can be used in any one week. Under pressure a sense of humour is required! It's a good thing for writers to be involved in other work around their *Archers* schedule, to refresh them, and in the end they must enjoy being creative as part of a team.'

So there it is – do you feel tempted to step into this demanding scene? There's no doubt it's wonderful experience if you can make the grade.

7. Features and Documentaries

Asa Briggs, the historian of British broadcasting, considers the pioneering development of the radio feature one of the BBC's greatest contributions to the art of radio. Until the 1950s BBC Radio had a separate Features Department, under the guidance of Laurence Gilliam, who gathered under his wing a band of the most distinguished radio-writers of the day. Legendary names such as D. G. Bridson, Louis MacNeice, Leonard Cotterell, Alan Burgess and W. R. Rodgers made the radio feature their own. Today dramatised features come under Drama Department, as do short stories, poetry, readings, and adaptations of books and translations. Documentary techniques are used in other departments, of course, to present a wide range of material.

What is a feature? It is hard to arrive at a definition, for a great variety of subjects and treatments can shelter under this umbrella, bordering on drama on the one side and illustrated talks on the other. The one clear distinction between features and plays seems to be that features deal with fact while plays deal with fiction. A play may dramatise a true story, but by the invention of imaginary dialogue and perhaps by juggling with the time-scale of real events for dramatic purposes, the writer creates a fictitious product. The feature writer, on the other hand, while employing many ingenious and original techniques of presentation, will be scrupulous to include in the script only material for which there is firm evidence, and to tell the story as it happened, eschewing the liberties of dramatic licence.

There is a category of programme lying between fiction and documentary which has come to be known as 'faction'. This is a sort of bastard form in which an account of true events is presented in a pseudo-documentary style, heightened by the inclusion of passages of imaginary dialogue. The listener does not know who is talking or on what authority, and by the end cannot tell how much of what he has heard is fact and how much fiction. I have a distaste for this category, and would urge radio writers to be rigorous in their rejection of it. Write a play, or write a feature, but don't confuse the two.

A good idea of the range of subjects and techniques which can be used can be found in the weekly *Kaleidoscope Feature* on BBC Radio 4, which deals with aspects of the arts.

The role of the narrator

Treatments at the feature-writer's disposal range from writers doing their own narration, with extracts from diaries and memoirs read by actors, through compilations of unscripted recordings, to full-scale dramatisations.

Being bound by the limitations of available documentation the features writer often needs a narrator. A linking voice can be used in a number of different ways. Narration may be written in an impersonal style to be read by an actor or professional presenter with the sort of neutral delivery that will not obtrude a personality into the programme. This sort of narrative provides a detached and authoritative commentary – the voice of the broadcasting station, as it were. A development of this is to use two alternating narrators with contrasting voices, a man and a woman perhaps. This can be a useful device for leavening long passages of factual exposition.

If the writer is a broadcaster the narration can be couched in the first person. This frees the writer to express personal opinions, provided it is made clear on what authority he or she is talking. You can approach the task of writing narration for yourself to speak in the same way as you would tackle writing a talk. A script which calls for only a limited use of other voices may be classed as an illustrated talk, and this can have implications for your contract and fee. See Chapter 12.

A third possibility is to put linking narrative into the mouth of one of the main characters in the programme. This can be very effective if suitable contemporary material is available in the form of a diary or letters. Letters, indeed, have formed the basis of many successful radio scripts, both documentary features and plays.

Duration

The preferred duration for full-scale features seems to be about forty-five minutes, but depending on the nature of the material and the time slot they may be longer or shorter. Many magazine programmes and news bulletins regularly include 'packages', short reports lasting five minutes or so, which usually consist of a compilation of unscripted interviews linked by narration. In collecting recordings for such reports the writer may wish to keep his own voice out of the programme. If he conducts the interviews skilfully it will be possible to edit out the questions, so that the results appear to be fluent statements by the interviewees. More guidance on interviewing techniques will be found in Chapter 9 on news and current affairs.

Anthologies, abridgements and adaptations

Under the heading 'features' we should also consider anthologies, abridgements and adaptations of existing works. There is an endless fund of themes around which anthologies can be built. Cats, ships and the sea, the English weather, the pleasures of gardening – the field is limitless. A particularly successful programme of this sort was an anthology of writings about the Devil, broadcast one Hallowe'en.

Full length novels are regularly abridged into fifteen-minute instalments for straight reading in such slots as *Womans Hour* or *A Book at Bedtime*. The writer in this case is faced with carrying out a surgical operation on the original work. First it has to be divided into the number of instalments agreed by the producer, with each part ending at a suitable point. Then each section must be pruned to exactly the right length. There may also be a requirement to write short summaries to be read by the announcer at intervals during the transmissions, to bring new listeners up to date in the story. As the original book must not be tampered with but simply shortened there is little creative satisfaction to be gained from this sort of work, and it is not particularly well paid.

Adaptations, however, are a different matter. Some of the best radio drama has come from adaptations of classic novels – Trollope's *Barchester* stories, Galsworthy's *Forsyte Saga*,

Herman Melville's *Moby Dick*, to mention only a few. Here the adapter has to soak himself in the original work and try to enter the mind of its author. The task is to recreate a work written for one medium, be it for the live theatre or the printed page, in terms of another – radio.

Adaptations of stage plays can be fairly straightforward, because the dialogue already exists. Dramatisations of novels, on the other hand, offer more complex problems. Even though the characters may be clearly delineated they have often been given far less actual dialogue than might be expected, and the adaptor has to take on the mantle of their original creator in order to make them talk.

Brian Sibley, adaptor of J.R.Tolkien's *Lord of the Rings*, has written eloquently about some of the problems he had to solve:

> Here are just a few facts about the first appearance in the book of some of the major characters (page numbers refer to the one-volume paperback edition): Frodo does not speak until p. 48 ('Has he [Bilbo] gone?'); Sam and Frodo do not appear together until the eavesdropping scene on p. 76; Merry has only two sentences until he meets his companions at the ferry on p. 110; and Gollum does not speak – apart from his reported exchange with Déagol – until p. 638!
>
> In order to resolve such difficulties – which would clearly be more of a problem for listeners who did not know the book – it seemed necessary to invent some passages of dialogue. A scene was written in which Sam delivers replies to the party invitations to Bilbo and Frodo at Bag End, and another in order to establish Merry before he sets out for Crickhollow. And as no-one can have failed to notice, the first episode began with the arrest of Gollum on the borders of Mordor and his subsequent interrogation in Barad-Dûr (an event reported by Gandalf and referred to in *Unfinished Tales*).

Here, for comparison, is the Merry/Frodo passage from the book and the script:

Book:

On September 20th, two covered carts went off laden to Buckland, conveying the furniture and goods that Frodo had not sold . . . The thought that he [Frodo] would so soon have to part with his young friends weighed on his heart. He wondered how he would break it to them . . .

The next morning they were busy packing another cart with the remainder of the luggage. Merry took charge of this, and drove off with Fatty . . . 'Someone must get there and warm the house before you arrive,' said Merry. 'Well, see you later – the day after tomorrow, if you don't go to sleep on the way!'

Script:

FRODO: Well, Merry, is everything ready?

MERRY: Yes: two cart-loads yesterday, full to overflowing, and now another one. I'm beginning to wonder if your new home will be big enough!

FRODO: Well, I've sold everything I could bear parting with to Lobelia, but some things I just had to take to remind me of Bilbo and Bag End.

MERRY: Well, I'd best be off . . . If I leave now I can get to Crickhollow and warm the house before you arrive – that is, if you're quite sure you want to walk rather than go by cart . . .

FRODO: Quite sure.

MERRY: Then I'll see you the day after tomorrow – if you don't go to sleep on the way!

FRODO: (LAUGHING) I'll try not to!

CART STARTS OFF, THEN STOPS

MERRY: (CALLING BACK) I'll tell you one thing, Frodo, you had better settle when you get to Buckland, because I for one am not helping you to move back again!

FRODO: What on earth makes you think Lobelia would ever sell Bag End back to me?

CART STARTS OFF ONCE MORE

MERRY: She might – at a profit! Farewell, Frodo – and good walking!

CART DRIVES OFF

FRODO: (TO HIMSELF) Poor Merry, what will you say when you learn the truth of all this?

FADE

Without offering any serious defence of additions of mock-Tolkien such as this, the astute reader will observe that, as well as helping establish Merry's light-hearted personality (he does not appear again until two episodes later), a variety of information is conveyed, ranging from details of where they are going and to whom Bag End has been sold, to a gentle reminder of the existence of Bilbo who left at the end of the previous episode.

Similar problems occur throughout the book. There are often a large number of characters present in a scene who do not make any contribution to the conversations taking place. When reading the book it matters very little if, for some pages, Gimli or Legolas don't speak, but on radio a silent character is a non-existent character. These difficulties come thickest at the end of the book: the struggle at the Crack of Doom between Frodo and Gollum is, we are told, enacted in silence (except for the odd hiss or two) which is hardly helpful to the would-be dramatist, and the final partings of the many characters are woefully short of dialogue. Consider, for example, Frodo's farewell to Sam: 'Then Frodo kissed Merry and Pippin, and last of all Sam, and went aboard . . .' Something more was needed for the final parting of the two heroes whose adventures we have followed for twenty-six weeks. Simple lines were given to Bilbo, Merry and Pippin, and for Sam and Frodo some dialogue was transferred from a page before:

FRODO: Sam . . .

SAM: Oh, Mr. Frodo, I thought you were going to enjoy the Shire for years and years, after all you have done.

FRODO: So I thought too, once. But I have been too deeply hurt, Sam. I tried to save the Shire, and it has been saved, but not for me. It must often be so, Sam, when things are in danger: someone has to give them up, lose them, so that others may keep them. But you are my heir: all that I had and might have had I leave to you, Sam. You will be the most famous gardener in history, and you will read things out of the Red Book, and keep alive the memory of the age that is gone, so that people will remember the Great Danger and so love their beloved land all the more. And that will keep you as busy and as happy as anyone can be, as long as your part of the story goes on . . .

SAM: Oh, Mr. Frodo, my dear . . . my dear . . .

THEY KISS

GANDALF: Now . . . Go in peace! I will not say: do not
           weep; for not all tears are an evil!

(Reprinted from an article in *Mallorn* 17, October 1981)

Although Brian Sibley claims that a silent character is a non-
existent character, it is worth recalling a play called *Congress*
by Malcolm Bradbury, produced for Afternoon Theatre in
November 1981. This centred on the experiences of a Dr Vestey
as a delegate to a European Congress to discuss cultural and
economic inter-penetration in the 1980s. Throughout the play
Dr Vestey himself never spoke. It was something of a tour-de-
force for both writer and producer, but not to my mind entirely
successful.

Copyright

Before embarking on making a radio adaptation of an existing
work it is as well to check on two important points. Firstly, is the
writer of the book, play or story still alive? If so, will he be happy
for you to adapt his work? He may well wish to do so himself. If
he has died within the past seventy years, copyright clearance will
have to be negotiated with the heirs of his estate. If you belong to
the Society of Authors they will be able to establish the copyright
situation for you. It is unlikely that you, as the writer, will have
to foot the bill for copyright payments; this will be the responsibility of the broadcasting company. It is wise, however, for you
to be fully informed as to whether copyright negotiations will be
necessary before you put up your script proposal.

Secondly, check with the broadcasting company to whom
you hope to sell your adaptation that they haven't already
produced a version of the same work before, or that they
haven't just commissioned someone else to make one. Quite
often the same notion can strike several writers and producers
at the same time.

Failure to make these essential checks can result in artistic
frustration and a lot of wasted work.

8. Comedy and Light Entertainment

In the days before radio and television, music-halls flourished up and down the country. Comedy acts were toured from one place to another round the various circuits. At each town the performers could expect a different audience, who would respond with spontaneous glee to material which, although already well-polished by use elsewhere, was entirely new to them. Those days are long over. A broadcast comedy show is heard by millions – the equivalent of more than a year's tour from town to town – at one go. The material is then old. No wonder the demand for good comedy writers is so voracious! The ability to see what will make people laugh, and then to set it down on paper, is a precious gift.

The old music-hall formula of a series of miscellaneous acts introduced by a wise-cracking compere has survived in television. Radio, however, has given birth to its own formats which, in the BBC, are the province of the Department of Light Entertainment. This department supplies a whole range of programmes to all four of the national radio networks. Most panel games, quizzes, sketch shows, revue and variety shows, and half-hour comedy series come from Light Entertainment. This department also has responsibility for half-hour cinema programmes such as 'Screenplay' and a few Cinema Features programmes.

The key thing to remember is that Light Entertainment Department thinks in terms of series. Any idea that may be submitted to them is assessed on whether or not it might make a series, and if possible a second and third series.

Nearly all series are of half-hour duration. This means in practice 29 minutes 30 seconds on Radio 4, and 29 minutes 15 seconds on Radio 2 including theme music and credits. It's a mistake to send in anything that lasts too long. Read your script aloud at a realistic speed, and cut it ruthlessly to the required length. If you can't, then perhaps you should send it to Drama Department instead.

30-minute comedy drama

Half-hour comedy drama programmes, often loosely called 'sit-com', call for a group of characters, more or less believable, to be placed in a situation more or less fantastical. The comedy arises from the interaction between the characters and each other, and the situations in which they find themselves. Sit-com is an aspect of drama, with laughs instead of tension. Each week the same characters recur, but the situation changes. In a play the protagonists develop and change as a result of the experiences they undergo; in sit-com they emerge just the same. The audience tunes in each week to hear them be themselves all over again.

One of the earliest sit-coms was *Bandwagon*, in which Arthur Askey purported to live in a flat on top of Broadcasting House with an assortment of characters including Nausea the goat. Then there was Tommy Handley with *ITMA*, and Jimmy Edwards in *Take it from Here*, with the continuing saga of the Glum family. Tony Hancock reached heights of genius in *Hancock's Half Hour*. More recently, we have had *King Street Junior*, set in a Primary school, and *Yes, Minister*, satirising the corridors of power and the machinery of government.

Depending on the nature of the scripts, they may or may not be produced before a live audience. The sort of comedy that produces hearty laughter usually needs the warmth of a human response when it is recorded. The warm-up man does his best to put the audience into a receptive frame of mind before recording starts, and to encourage its members to see themselves as actively contributing to the success of the show, as indeed they do. The mirth you hear punctuating broadcasts of BBC comedy shows is spontaneous and not canned. Shows which rely on a more intellectual approach, tending to evoke quiet chuckles rather than guffaws, are better off without an audience.

The elements of comedy

Structure is even more important in a series comedy than in a play. Every episode, and every scene within an episode, must build cumulatively for laughs, starting with a chuckle and ending with a belly laugh that will carry the audience over into the next scene. Successful comedy is created either by performers who are naturally funny, or by straight actors with a good sense of comic timing. Both groups need scripts in order to be able to work their magic. The trick is either to put a funny man in an ordinary situation, or to put an ordinary man in an extraordinary situation. In each case, the juxtaposition of the character with the situation leads to anarchy, and all good comedy partakes to some extent of anarchy.

Perhaps the supreme example of comic anarchy can be found in the *Goon Show*, originally broadcast between 1951 and 1960, but still brought out of honourable retirement from time to time for nostalgic repeat airings, and still capable of reducing its audience to helplessness. The *Goon Show* team had the advantage of naturally funny men, all capable of playing a number of different parts with highly characteristic voices, plus brilliant scripts written by themselves.

A number of the *Goon Show* scripts have been published in book form, and the writer can learn much from their short lines, economy of language, consistent and clear cut presentation of the various characters, exploitation of catch-phrases, surrealistic use of effects, and the zany logic which somehow succeeds in creating the radio equivalent of a drawing by Escher. The Goons achieved a level of sublime lunacy which has rarely been equalled.

Panel games and quizzes

Quizzes and panel games are another important element of the Light Entertainment output. These fall into two main categories:

1) Straightforward quizzes, in which opposing teams, often drawn from members of the public, compete with each other to answer general knowledge questions. This type of programme relies for its interest on the competitive excitement of whether or not the teams can answer the questions accurately within the time allowed. **Examples:** *Round Britain Quiz, Top of the Form*.

2) Entertainment quizzes and games, which rely on show-business personalities to divert the audience with amusing anecdotes and chat while answering the questions, which are only incidental to the main business of the programme. **Examples:** *Brain of Britain, The News Quiz, Just a Minute.*

Devising a successful quiz-game format can be a paying proposition, and good ideas for new programmes will be welcomed. *Twenty Questions,* a radio version of an old-time parlour game, was so successful that it ran for years and years, making the reputations of several broadcasting personalities, and a lot of money for its creator. Before you submit a new inspiration, however, check on the following points:

a) Is it really original?
b) Does it contain more than a proposal for one round within a programme?
c) Does it ask too much of the contributors? The tasks you want the panellists to undertake should be interesting and entertaining in themselves, and not rely too much on the sparkling chat of the participants – who may, even the best of them, have an off day.

These are among the main reasons for the rejection of suggestions in this field of programming.

Sketches and 'quickies'

If you want to write sketches and 'quickies', study the current output and decide which programmes attract you. By the time a programme is broadcast the whole series will probably have already been recorded, so the likelihood of your being able to contribute to the current series is remote. Your best course is to approach the producer, whose name will be in *Radio Times*, and find out if another series is planned, and if so whether there is scope for outside contributions. For very topical shows such as *Week Ending* and *The News Huddlines*, which do indeed use a lot of material from freelance writers, it is more or less essential to live close to the production centre, so that you can attend script meetings and send in specially tailored material at the last minute. There is a

Wednesday lunch-time meeting at Broadcasting House geared
to *Week Ending* which is open to absolutely anybody who
wants to write topical comedy.

Producers in Light Entertainment apply what they call the
'tick test' to new scripts – there has to be at least one laugh per
page. Another approach is to study the work of any comic you
particularly admire, put together a batch of short items, and
send them to him, with a covering letter saying you would like
to write material for him. If he comes to perform in your neigh-
bourhood go to his show, and call on him in his dressing room
afterwards. He cannot but be pleased at your interest. Personal
contact is worth a lot in show business, enthusiasm and
perseverance even more.

Find a partner

Writing comedy is hard work, and lonelier than most forms of
writing. As you polish and rework the lines it is easy to become
discouraged and cease to believe that anyone could ever find
them funny. A fellow-writer with a similar sense of humour
could provide the necessary antidote – someone to laugh at
your jokes, to spark you off, to come up with another idea
when your mind is a blank. Many superb comedy scripts have
been written by partnerships. Muir and Norden, Galton and
Simpson, Perry and Crofts, Brady and Bingham are names to
conjure with in the business. Perhaps a like-minded colleague
might be the answer for you. How do you find one? Join the
nearest Writers' Circle.

Write to the BBC Radio Light Entertainment Department
and ask for their guidelines for writers. They will send you an
invaluable hand-out listing what they want, and what they
don't want, and giving information about how to set out scripts
and how to submit material.

9. News and Current Affairs

From the earliest days of broadcasting the presentation of up-to-date news has been a major element of radio programming. The capacity to be truly topical gives radio a marked advantage over all other media. Newspapers have to be typeset, printed and distributed. Even television, with its more cumbersome equipment, can only match the flexibility of radio by luck or careful pre-planning. The radio reporter needs no more than a telephone to feed his story directly into the middle of a news bulletin. Eye and voice are the tools of his trade, closely supported by his trusty tape-recorder. The best way in to this profession is through journalistic training coupled with experience gained by contributing to local newspapers.

Balance and impartiality

Who decides what is news, and how it should be presented? In Britain the law relating to broadcasting requires that news shall be presented with impartiality and objectivity. The BBC's licence includes the words:

> The Corporation shall at all times refrain from sending any broadcast matter expressing the opinion of the Corporation on current affairs or on matters of public policy . . .

So, unlike newspapers, broadcasting companies are not permitted to take an editorial line. At one time an attempt was made to balance opposing points of view on controversial topics within individual programmes. This was found to be virtually impossible, and now opposing points of view are presented in different programmes balanced over the output as a whole. Politicians often claim, especially at election times, that the BBC or IRN News is biased against them, but so long as all parties feel equally strongly that they have been the victims the broad-casters believe they have steered a reasonably fair course.

Writing the news

Who actually writes the news? The task is shared between reporters at the coal-face, as it were, and newsroom staff who edit and may rewrite a story to fit constraints of time or policy. Many radio journalists start as 'stringers' – local correspondents who telephone the newsroom with a report of an event in their area. Their material may be written up for the news-reader to deliver and their voices never heard on the air. On the other hand, they may find themselves at the heart of a major news story, called on for eyewitness accounts for a whole range of different bulletins, each of which will need a different length and a different style. Compare *News at One* on Radio 4 with *Newsbeat* on Radio 1, or the news as presented on your Local Radio Station, BBC or Independent.

An internal News Guide produced by the BBC for its own staff points out that 'It is a waste of time to broadcast news unless it is listened to and understood . . . Our aim is intelligibility, and what is more, immediate intelligibility.' It goes on to recommend 'a style that is crisp, economical, direct and colloquial, but not slangy or slap-dash, relaxed yet precise. We prefer the short word to the long one, the simple sentence to the complex, the concrete to the abstract, the direct statement to the inverted sentence. We do not write for pedants. But we shun journalese.'

Two books which may be especially helpful in connection with news and current affairs writing are R. W. Burchfield's *The Spoken Word, A BBC Guide* and *The Complete Plain Words* by Sir Ernest Gowers, revised by Sidney Greenbaum and Janet Whitcut.

News versus comment

Ideally, a distinction should be made between news – what actually happened – and comment, which is a response to or interpretation of what happened. In practice it is extremely difficult to draw a line between the two. The very selection of items for inclusion in a bulletin and the order in which they are placed constitutes comment of a sort. It behoves the radio journalist to be scrupulously careful in choice of vocabulary not to imply any sort of judgement where none is intended. A word such as 'freedom fighter' carries an overtone of approval, while 'terrorist' suggests the opposite. 'Gunman' might serve for either. To say 'Troops were forced to open fire' is to imply a subjective opinion that there was no alternative. 'Troops opened fire' is a neutral statement.

Meticulous accuracy is essential in all reporting, and this extends to sources and attributions. 'The Labour/Conservative group on the Council have succeeded in convincing their opponents of the necessity . . .' might more accurately be reported as 'The Labour/Conservative group on the Council *say* they have succeeded in convincing . . .'. If 'say' were replaced by 'maintain', or 'assert', or 'claim', any of these alternative words would carry its own connotation of credibility – or the reverse.

Interviews

Interviews form an important element in news reports. The reporter's task is to use skill with words to set a scene and bring it to life for the listener, and then to avoid the limelight by eliciting as much of the story as possible from the key people involved.

Interviewing is both a skill and an art. The interviewer must have a clear idea of the purpose of the recording and the length of time it will eventually be allowed to run. Interviews in news bulletins usually have to be short and to the point. The reporter must evoke factual responses and avoid leading questions which allow simple 'yes' or 'no' replies. Thus, not:

Q. Mr. Jones, I believe you were standing in the doorway when the thunderbolt fell?
A. Yes.

but:

Q. Mr. Jones, where were you when the thunderbolt fell?
A. Standing in the doorway . . .

In slotting a recording into the rest of the programme the interviewer's first question is often cut. The extract above might be introduced as follows:

NEWSREADER: A thunderbolt struck a shop in Little
Mudhampton this morning. Our reporter
asked Fred Jones the shopkeeper where he
was when it fell.
TAPE INSERT: 'Standing in the doorway . . .

Some interviewees are fluent talkers. One question unleashes a
graphic description of their experiences. Others have to be
prompted. Never, never comment. Avoid remarks such as 'How
interesting', 'Did it really', or 'No!' A radio interview is not a
social conversation. Instead of reacting as if it were, the interviewer should simply go on to the next question.

Be careful not to interrupt your interviewee as this will make
for difficult editing. You may want to eliminate your own voice
from the final version and present the answers to a series of
questions as a continuous statement. If you both speak at once
this will be impossible.

The purpose of the interview may not be a topical report for a
news bulletin. Perhaps it is a profile of someone in the public eye,
and time has been allocated for an extended 'personality' piece.
Now, although the forgoing remarks still apply, you can afford
to be more leisurely in your approach. Research your subject
thoroughly beforehand. Plan an over-all structure, with a good
opening and close. Prepare a list of questions. If possible, get to
know your interviewee beforehand and gain his confidence.
Agree the areas to be covered in your discussion, but never
under any circumstances rehearse. If you do, you may find your
interviewee trying to remember what he said last time, or using
expressions such as 'Well, as I said before . . .' You may want
to make a short trial recording to check microphone balance,
but ask a totally unconnected question such as 'What did you
have for breakfast this morning?'.

There are several ways of encouraging people to go on
talking into a tape recorder, but they have to be non-verbal.
You must not say 'Yes?', 'Mmm?', or 'Go on'. Your best tool
is eye-contact. Rivet your victim with your fascinated gaze
and convince him that you are deeply interested in what he is
saying. As long as you nod enthusiastically at intervals he will
go on elaborating his story. When he comes to a halt, just
remain silently expectant. People find it very difficult not to
fill a silence, and probably something more will be forth-

coming. If your tape has pauses in it you can edit them out afterwards.

On the whole it is wiser not to play recordings back to people after they have been interviewed. Often time does not allow for this, but even if it does people are sometimes dissatisfied with recordings and you may find yourself pressed to re-do the whole thing, or cut various passages – perhaps the very ones which you feel to be most effective. This is not to say that answers to some questions should not be re-recorded at the request of either interviewer or interviewee. When you come to edit the recording, integrity requires that you present what your interviewee said in the light that he intended, using your professional skill and judgement to compile the most effective end product.

Commentating

Radio's capacity to bring the listener reports of events while they are actually happening has led to the rise of the professional commentator. Ball-by-ball accounts of cricket matches and the thrills of Wimbledon tennis are regularly relayed in word pictures to the listening millions. Associated noises – the thwack of ball on bat or racket, the roar of the crowd – add to the impression of actuality, but the main burden falls on the speaker's voice. This is even more true of ceremonial public occasions such as the opening of Parliament, Trooping the Colour, or a Royal Wedding. The commentator has to keep talking, come what may.

Successful commentaries require immense and detailed preparation. All those long minutes when nothing is happening – the batsman is walking out to the wicket, the start of the race is delayed, the Royal carriage has not yet appeared – must be filled with colourful and appropriate talk. The commentator must become familiar with every relevant fact, so that it can be dropped it in at some empty and unforgiving moment. When the action resumes the commentator must become a sort of tap from which an account of the passing scene pours like water, bringing the listener vivid vicarious experience. He must share in and communicate the excitement of the occasion, but remain sufficiently in command of himself to be articulate and lucid.

Over the years commentators have come to use a technique called the Pyramid Method – clearly expounded in Brian Johnson's book *My Friends the Commentators*. The Commentator starts his broadcast at the tip of the pyramid by giving immediately the main essentials of the situation. Then, gradually as the broadcast continues, he can broaden outwards by adding less important but still relevant information. In quiet pauses in the flow of events the commentator can draw on what is called 'associative' material – the history of the occasion, the significance of the uniforms, or perhaps a personal anecdote.

He should, nevertheless, remember to weave in a description of the scene again from time to time, and repeat essential information, such as the current score in a cricket or football match, for the benefit of new listeners who may have just tuned in.

Two important 'don'ts' for commentators – never admit you can't see even if it's true, and don't take sides. Your listeners will include people of all sympathies and nationalities.

Brian Johnson tells the story of the ace Canadian commentator Stewart MacPherson preparing for a broadcast on a firework display by filling a blank sheet of paper with every adjective he thought he might want to use – brilliant, fantastic, magnificent, sparkling, and so-on. As the display went on he struck each adjective out as he used it, and so cut down on the inevitable repetitions.

If you dream of becoming a sports commentator you could start by writing up reports of matches for a school magazine or local newspaper. You could practice by watching a match on television with the sound turned down, and recording your own commentary. Play the tape back later, and see how much of a sound picture you gave of what actually happened. Then tackle the sports editor at your local radio station to see if he will give you a trial.

The best commentators sometimes get carried away in the stress of the moment, and the satirical magazine *Private Eye* has immortalised one of them by producing anthologies of some of their wilder malapropisms under the title *Colemanballs*. One of my favourites – not, as it happens, by David Coleman – is reproduced overleaf.

'*If our swimmers want to win any more medals, they'll have
to put their skates on.*'

DAVE BRENNER

Colemanballs III (Private Eye/André Deutsch)

10. Radio for Children

Between the dark and the daylight,
When the night is beginning to lower,
Comes a pause in the day's occupations
That is known as the children's hour.

These lines by Longfellow gave a title to the first radio programmes specially for children, which grew up in parallel with but quite separate from broadcasts for schools. Throughout the golden age of radio the time between 5.0 pm and the six o'clock news was dominated by programmes for younger listeners. *Childrens Hour* was a microcosm of BBC output as a whole. Stories, music, quizzes and competitions, plays and features of top quality were produced by organisers in each of the seven main BBC regions.

Childrens Hour became a marvellous proving ground for broadcasters of all sorts. Fees were lower than those offered for contributions to the rest of the output, and some of the finest productions were achieved on shoe-string budgets, through real dedication on the part of producers, writers and performers.

The audience was just as dedicated, and included a large number of adult devotees. This is not surprising when one considers what they were offered. Dramatisations of all the classic children's books, including *Wind in the Willows*, *Winnie the Pooh* and *The House at Pooh Corner*, lots of Dickens and Kipling, John Masefield's *Box of Delights* and Frances Hodgson Burnett's *The Secret Garden*, original plays by writers such as Geoffrey Household, Kathleen Fidler and Geoffrey Trease, and immortal creations such as *Toytown* and *Worzel Gummidge*.

But society was changing. Children were staying up later, mothers were going out to work. The days of nannies and nursery tea were long over. Television had arrived, and young listeners were becoming viewers, or choosing their radio fare from the general output. In 1964 the axe fell, and the BBC abolished *Childrens Hour*. Some have never forgiven this act of vandalism.

Thirty years later BBC radio programmes for children are still in limbo. There were for a time experimental runs of a programme called *Cats Whiskers* in the mornings during school holidays. Unfortunately an audience is more easily killed off than re-established, and *Cats Whiskers* did not survive. Then a ray of hope arrived in the shape of Radio 5. The first brief for this new network was to carry children's and youth programmes, and this is did with considerable success. However, in 1994 Radio 5 was handed over entirely to News and Sport, with the result that programmes for children and schools found themselves without a home. They are at present being shoe-horned in to Radio 3 and Radio 4, but this is hardly the right way to build a consistent audience, or, one would think, the way to build a radio audience for the future.

Some of the famous successes of the past have been dug out and repeated, or produced anew – *Wind in the Willows*, *The Box of Delights*, *The Secret Garden*, and there is a slot early on Sunday evenings which is being labelled 'Childrens Radio 4'. It has carried a serialisation of *The Horse and his Boy* by C. S. Lewis, from his *Chronicles of Narnia*. It is to be hoped that this slot at least will be treated consistently for long enough to create a loyal audience.

It does seem ironic that, while both BBC and Independent Television make generous provision for children and some local radio stations take account of the interests of their younger listeners, the BBC national networks, flagship of all that is best in world radio, steadfastly refuse to do so.

A programme that was originally planned for an adult audience but hit the jackpot with older children was *Dick Barton, Special Agent*, first broadcast in 1946. Geoffrey Webb and Neil Tuson's book *The Inside Story of Dick Barton* gives some interesting insights into the birth and development of this fifteen minute daily adventure serial. When parents and teachers began to realise that schoolchildren were glued to their radio sets at 6.45 pm instead of getting on with their homework all sorts of concerns began to be voiced as to the undesirable influences that Dick Barton might be exerting. It was a straightforward entertainment programme, and therefore not subject to any of the restraints which might have been imposed by a School Broadcasting Council sub-committee. The production team nevertheless found that they had to take careful account of the fact that the broadcasts went straight into the heart of people's homes, where they were lapped up like mother's milk by a young and impressionable audience. A code of conduct was devised to which the writers learned meticulously to adhere. Here are the 'Thirteen commandments':

1. Barton is intelligent as well as hard-hitting.
2. He uses force only when normal peaceful means have failed.
3. Barton never commits an offence under the criminal code, no matter how desirable the end may be to justify the means.
4. In reasonable circumstances Barton may deceive, but he never lies.
5. Barton's violence is restricted to clean socks on the jaw. Refinements of unarmed combat tried by British Commandos cannot be practised by him or his colleagues.
6. His enemies have more latitude in behaviour, but may not inflict any injury or punishment which is basically sadistic.
7. Barton and his colleagues do not wittingly involve members of the public in circumstances which would cause them distress.
8. Barton has given up drink altogether.
9. Sex plays no part in his adventures. He has no flirtations or affairs, and his enemies have no 'molls' or mistresses.
10. Political themes are unpopular as well as being occasionally embarrassing.
11. Horrific effects must be closely watched. Supernatural or pseudo-supernatural sequences involving ghosts, night-prowling gorillas, vampires and so on should be avoided.
12. Swearing may not be used by any character.
13. Neither Barton and his colleagues, nor his opponents may use cut-throat razors, or any other sharp instrument commonly found in private houses, for the purpose of causing injury, or for intimidation.

This is probably a fairly sound code for writing material for a school-age audience even in the 1990s, though nowadays one would need, sadly, to add an extra admonition concerning drugs.

Local radio stations, both BBC and ILR, are interested in attracting young listeners, and many stations run stories, phone-ins, quizzes, competitions and games, with a liberal mixture of pop music, specially designed for the younger members of the audience. Ideas for contributions to these programmes which fit the style of the station will undoubtedly be received with interest.

Participation is a great audience-puller, and children respond quickly to programmes which they recognise as being specially directed to them. They develop a fiercely possessive attitude towards them, and listen with critical appreciation. *Childrens Hour* always had a massive postbag, full of all sorts of comments, complaints and requests. To those who are concerned for the quality of radio, a committed audience seems to be the most important factor in assuring a flourishing future. Surely, above all, it is important to nourish and encourage that audience while it is young.

The commercial world of audio-publishing has been quick to recognise the demand among children for stories to be read aloud. Every supermarket carries a display of childrens audio-cassettes, and aspiring writers of children's stories could do worse than approach some of the production companies involved.

Children 2000

It is good to hear that the campaign group Children 2000 is flying the flag anew for children's radio, launching a unique scheme to develop a national radio network for children, with a view to investing Lottery funds. Code-named 'SoundStart' the project is based on evidence that a varied radio diet is essential for children's leisure listening and can play a vital part in the early learning of basic skills.

A series of Restricted Service Licences (RSLs) in selected inner city and rural areas will form 'sound platforms' for the development of a 'Listen, Learn and Play' curriculum. Each RSL will offer 28 days of fun and games, music, song, story and rhyme, and promote shared listening between parents and children to encourage imagination, concentration, talking, reading and writing, caring and sharing in Britain's youngest citizens. Older children will also have an important part to play both as listeners and broadcasters. Air time is to be given to their creative work, and also for their opinions to be more widely heard on a variety of issues that concern them, with special emphasis on their aspirations for the Millennium.

SoundStart is shortly to carry out a Digital Audio Broadcasting (DAB) trial aimed at children under 8 years old, a world first for children, to be followed by a month-long RSL for London. After the premiere SoundStart plans to move out as a road show to cover areas of greatest need. It is intended that the pilot RSLs will form the basis for a national children's network.

This initiative, which has all-party parliamentary support, has been described by Baroness Warnock as 'inspired and prudent use of public resources to serve a national need.'

One cannot but hope that the efforts of everyone concerned, and especially those of Susan Stranks (co-founder of Children 2000) may be crowned with success.

11. Educational and Information Programmes

The potential of radio as a medium of education was recognised early. By 1926 nearly 2000 schools in Britain were listening to radio programmes. School broadcasting was not, however, greeted with unmixed enthusiasm. There were a number of worries, including the fear that radio might supplant the classroom teacher and lead to loss of jobs in the profession. This was ironic, because it quickly became apparent that school broadcasts depended closely on co-operation at the receiving end for their success. Listening to the radio was not an easy option for the teacher.

The BBC was anxious for advice from the educational world on how to proceed, and in 1927 the Carnegie Trustees financed a major enquiry in collaboration with the Kent Advisory Committee of Teachers and the Kent Education Committee. The famous 'Kent Experiment' resulted in a report called 'Educational Broadcasting' which has had an enduring influence on policy.

Essential partnership

The most important point to emerge was the necessity of establishing a close partnership between broadcasters and educationists. This led to the setting up of the School Broadcasting Council which, through a network of sub-committees, was to 'commission' the BBC to provide broadcasts designed to fulfil clearly defined purposes for different target audiences. In other words, the BBC would plan its educational output in response to direct requests from representative advisory bodies.

This principle still holds good, and leads to the corollary that, certainly in national network radio, all educational material is commissioned.

A second key recommendation was that broadcasting should concentrate on offering the audience material and experiences which could not be provided by the teacher in the classroom. Although the press might refer to 'lessons on the air' the BBC School Broadcasting Department leaned over backwards to dispel notions that it was providing any such thing. The radio was seen as providing an extra resource for the teacher, a stimulus to the imagination, which could be drawn on to enrich the normal curriculum. The teacher's role in the classroom was paramount, and nothing would be done to usurp it.

There have been many developments and changes since the early days of school radio. Perhaps the most important of these have been the arrival of television and the advent of commercially funded broadcasting. ITV in fact was ahead of the BBC in starting a television service for schools in 1957, now co-ordinated by Channel 4. Another key development has been the introduction of new recording technologies making it possible to time-shift programmes so that they do not have to be listened to or viewed at the time they are broadcast. This has had a dramatic effect on the ways in which broadcasts are planned and used.

The BBC has always been a major player in the educational field, and in 1993 BBC Education was launched as a separate Directorate, encompassing radio, television and educational publishing across the full range of formal and continuing education. The School Broadcasting Council was merged with the Continuing Education Advisory Council to become the Educational Broadcasting Council.

It is BBC policy to place educational and informative programmes at the heart of its schedules, and it has announced its intention to make the best use of terrestrial, cable and satellite, Video, Audio, CD-ROM and other main non-broadcast options.

One lesson which has been learned by the broadcasters is that radio on its own is a bird with a broken wing. It needs support, perhaps from printed publications, or from computer software, or ideally from a real live teacher who can help and stimulate. The techniques of distance-learning are highly effective over limited periods of time, but the spirit takes fire with human contact and encouragement.

Qualifications for educational broadcasters

It is not essential to be a trained teacher in order to write educational programmes. It is important, however, to know and understand the audience for whom you are writing, and to be familiar with current educational thinking and practice in the appropriate subject area. In presenting new information and ideas you must know what your audience has already learned, and put over your material in terms that they will understand.

If you find yourself wanting to use an expression that will be unfamiliar to them, various alternatives present themselves. First, ask yourself what the main objective is of this particular broadcast, and whether it is essential for this expression to be used at this point in the course. If not, find a way of rephrasing your script so as to avoid it, otherwise you run the risk of blocking understanding of the rest of what you are saying. If your listeners do need to learn it, you can either explain it there and then, or make sure, through supporting printed notes, that an explanation will have been given to them before they hear the broadcast.

The schools audience is particularly rewarding for two reasons. Firstly, you will be given a clear brief to work to, so you will know exactly what the broadcast is intended to achieve. Secondly, there will be positive feedback afterwards from the listening end. This is somewhat different from the general output, where – unless you have a sensational hit or a scandal on your hands – you may wonder who, if anyone, listened to your broadcast at all.

The educational broadcasting output receives only limited coverage in *Radio Times*. The BBC Directorate of Education produces separate catalogues on forthcoming resources to be provided in radio, television and published form for its principle audiences – Primary, Secondary, Adult Education and Languages. These can be obtained via BBC Educational Information at White City, London.

Openings for freelances

Any educational broadcast is the fruit of a long period of gestation. It is largely a waste of time to send in unsolicited scripts designed as part of the current output. Decisions may have been taken to scrap or modify an established series, or to introduce something new and different. What you are listening to now was almost certainly commissioned some time ago. Nevertheless, not everything is sewn up tight. There are openings for freelance contributions, and producers are glad to hear from people interested in writing for an educational audience. If you want to contribute to educational radio, write to the producer of a series which interests you, or to the Chief Education Officer for Continuing Education and Training, or the Chief Education Officer for Schools Programmes. State your interest and experience with the audience, and enclose a sample of your work. This need not be anything written for radio, so long as it gives an impression of the quality of your writing.

The Open University

The BBC Open University Production Centre at Milton Keynes was set up to produce the radio and television components of all the Open University courses. In addition it has now gained a considerable reputation as a national resource for the origination of audio-visual training materials, and is rapidly developing special expertise in the field of inter-active media such as CD-ROM. Medical Schools in particular have taken advantage of this special area of excellence.

Educational radio in the wider world

The BBC's knowledge and expertise in the field of educational broadcasting is in demand throughout the world, and many foreign institutions send students to this country for BBC training courses. This country is fortunate in being well provided with good schools and trained teachers. It can afford to regard the broadcasting media almost as a luxury, to be used or not as educationists may choose. In third world countries, however, where schools are scattered and ill equipped and perhaps even the teachers have only had a limited education, radio is a vital resource. Broadcasting can spread understanding of new farming techniques, health education, and many more topics of vital interest in helping developing communities to achieve fuller and happier lives.

In developed countries with western traditions, such as Australia and New Zealand, Radio is also a life-line over long distances. Educational programmes, both for school children and adults, are an important part of broadcasting output. In Australia 'Schools of the Air' are run by each state for children in isolated communities. Teachers at central studios teach their far-flung classes by two-way conversation, using the technology of interactive radio.

Religious broadcasting

Radio is a powerful selling medium, and its capacity to put over a message has been exploited for good and ill. It has been used to sell soap-powder and Fascism, to convey information and to preach religious creeds. The development of radio has coincided with great changes in education and society. When the BBC started broadcasting in the 1920s, religion to most of its listeners meant Christianity. The daily service and *Thought for the day* remain as reminders of that state of affairs. Religious broadcasting in today's multi-cultural society has a much wider connotation. A religious affairs producer may commission plays, features, or talks and discussions of all sorts, reflecting all the principal faiths now being practised in this country and around the world. Ideas from thoughtful writers will find a warm response in this field. Local radio plays a particularly important part in religious broadcasting, and the speakers are not only vicars and priests. Many distinguished speakers and producers have graduated to national networks from the proving ground of low-budget local radio programmes. Limitations often provide the best stimulus for truly creative and imaginative work, and this is certainly true in the field of religious affairs.

Writing commercials

It may seem surprising to put commercials into a chapter on education and information, but the radio commercial is one of the most tightly packaged information capsules it is possible to create. Compared with TV, press and posters, radio commercials are a relatively cheap advertising medium, both in cost of production and in buying the media time. Therefore they attract advertisers of all sorts, and at first they were regarded as the domain of the local advertiser. But the arrival of national commercial radio stations, coupled with the power of advertising, with its addictive following by the big client companies and their agents, simply perpetuates the very act of 'having to advertise'. So advertising is now an inevitable part of our lives, and the role of the writer is a very responsible one.

Because radio is still considered to be 'a cheap medium' the writer has the opportunity to develop quirky ideas, at relatively low cost to the patron. Advertising's ability to intrigue and amuse has always played a strong part in its ability to survive the recessionary axe. Radio, given its cost, is no exception.

Writing commercials calls for imagination, skill, and immense discipline. There is a key message that must be conveyed in, say, thirty seconds, and all the skills described in other chapters of this book may be called upon in putting the message over effectively. Whatever the product may be, its name must remain in the minds of potential purchasers, and it must be associated with the right image. Commercials vary widely in their approaches, from the catchy jingle and the straight sell in one speaker's voice to a mini-drama. Yes – it *is* possible to have a mini-drama inside these tight confines, especially if the characters are drawn from a well-known comedy show already established on the air. A series of airline advertisements featuring Ronnie Barker was a good example.

With situation or story-based commercials, there is the opportunity to create sequels or sagas. The story can move from episode to episode, even to the point of being heard in several consecutive slots, without boring the audience. On the contrary, they should hanker for the next instalment. If this sounds like the Nescafe Gold Blend device, remember that saga played itself out through episode one for three months, to the point of boredom, and only then did they give us episode two. Imagine what could happen with a 30 spot package over a week on Classic FM!

The first thing to bear in mind if you want to write commercials is, what life is like from the consumer's end. Advertisements are aimed at ordinary men and women – people like yourself – and as the writer you have to act as a go-between for the consumer and the advertiser. Empathising with your target audience and understanding exactly who they are is every bit as important in writing a radio commercial as in scripting a school broadcast.

This target audience will not be receptive to the product every time a commercial is broadcast – families do not buy three-piece suites and airline tickets to New York every day of the week. But by creating an entertaining advertisement you will build up a favourable attitude to the product, ensuring that when the moment comes to buy whatever it is, your product's name comes to the consumer's mind with agreeable assoc-iations. The commercial should please listeners in some way or other so that they enjoy hearing it repeatedly, even when it is not relevant to their current needs. When it does become relevant the goodwill it has generated over a period of time will pay dividends, and your product will have a head-start over its unadvertised – or poorly advertised – rivals.

Advertisers frequently refer to the USP – the Unique Selling Proposition. Try to analyse the product you are writing about along these lines:

Unique: What is special about this product that marks it out from others?

Selling: What is the benefit that this product confers that will make people want to buy it?

Proposition: How can you present this special benefit, in a distinctive and memorable manner, so that potential purchasers can appreciate its advantages *through their ears alone?*

We are back to the three key points emphasised in the intro-duction to this book, which are valid whatever field of radio you choose to work in.

Audio visual scripts

An interesting spin-off from educational radio in the 1960s was dubbed 'radiovision'. A radiovision programme was a sound track designed to be complemented by a set of slides or a filmstrip. The sound track was broadcast and recorded at the receiving end; the slides were ordered separately. Schools could then replay the tape and project the accompanying pictures simultaneously, in their own time. This was not the same thing as the simultaneous broadcasting of a television programme on sound radio, which has also been called radio-vision.

The hybrid tape-slide medium has valuable advantages over both radio and television for certain applications. Projected slides can provide bigger, better pictures for a class than the television screen. Both television and film abhor a still picture, whereas a slide can be held on the screen for as long as may be desirable. Visual material in a programme can be updated cheaply and easily by substituting fresh slides. In programmes dealing with historical subjects slides can often show actual contemporary pictures, whereas television or film producers may be driven to resort to reconstructions or library footage which may not be authentic.

One of the most notable examples of this was a radiovision programme first broadcast thirty or more years ago called *In the Trenches*. The script, by John Chilton, told the story of the First World War through quotations from letters, poems, memoirs, and above all the popular songs sung by the soldiers themselves. The filmstrip showed posters, newspaper reports, and actual contemporary photographs of daily life in the trenches. The interplay between the black humour of the soldiers' ballads with their relentlessly cheerful tunes and the grim images of the muddy carnage in Flanders resulted in an experience of overwhelming irony and pathos. Truly the whole was far greater than the sum of its parts. This school history programme achieved immortality in fresh incarnations on stage and screen as *Oh What a Lovely War!*

In the Trenches was a simple programme in which a single projector was used, and the film-strip frames changed by hand. If extra projectors are brought in and a computer employed to synchronise them with the sound-track a sophisticated result can be achieved which is very close to moving-picture film. Slides can be mixed, dissolved, superimposed and split-screened with dazzling virtuosity. The advertising world has taken this technique to its heart, and elaborate 'audio-visuals' to extol the virtues of new products and services are now a recognised element of glossy PR presentations. Many museums, art galleries and stately homes now offer visitors recorded commentaries to listen to as they go round, or an audio-visual programme to stop and view at some stage of their tour. The techniques of writing these are similar to those of writing a radio script.

Script-writing methods

In writing an audio-visual script it is important to achieve a balance between pictures and talk. Which should come first, the slides or the commentary? This question is often asked, and the answer is that they have to come together. Start with a blank A4 page, divided vertically in two. Down the left-hand side list the pictures you have, or hope to obtain. In the right-hand half, set down the proposed commentary. If you find yourself with a full page of speech and only one picture to go with it there is something wrong with your script. Modify the commentary, add some more pictures, and establish a close interplay between sound and vision.

How to signal the change from one slide to the next can offer problems. A distinctive sound can be used, such as the 'ting' of a bell; or you can write the signal into the script, and get your commentator to say 'Now move on to slide 4', or something similar. On the other hand, if your programme is not openly didactic but designed to convey an aesthetic experience this sort of instruction destroys any atmosphere you may have built up. The alternative is to supply the user with a detailed copy of the script with clear instructions as to the slide changes. Electronic synchronisers are available which will put pulses on the magnetic tape, thus ensuring that the slides are changed automatically at the right points,and for more elaborate presentations computerised installations will be brought into play.

Tape-slide programmes are well-suited to self access use, and many educational libraries have booths where students can work individually with this sort of material. Visualise how your audience will eventually use the script you are working on, and if appropriate write in instructions such as 'Now switch off, and work through the next example. Switch on again when you are ready.'

This book does not set out to deal with visual presentation, but one point should be remembered when choosing illustrations for slide-tape programmes: select landscape-shape pictures rather than those of upright format. It's a small point, but one that is often overlooked, and makes a great deal of difference to the finished result.

The medium of tape and slide has been enthusiastically adopted by the world of advertising and public relations, and is frequently used in prestige presentations such as the launch of a new car model. If you are interested in writing for this market, try approaching an independent radio production company. (See addresses in Appendix II.)

12. Markets, Fees and Copyright

All writers who want to be paid for their work have to learn how to market it, and be prepared to spend time doing so. Marketing means more than just salesmanship. It means identifying a possible purchaser, finding out exactly what that purchaser usually buys, tailoring your product to fit the specification, and presenting it in as attractive and professional a way as possible.

If you want to write for radio there is no substitute for listening to the way successful people have done it. Plays, short stories and comedy programmes are available on tape, and in some cases the scripts have been published in book form as well. Try listening to a tape and following the written text at the same time. This not only illustrates different writing techniques, it reveals the contribution skilled acting can make in lifting bare words off the page and bringing a situation to life.

Looking for possible markets

This book has been written from the standpoint of the United Kingdom, where the BBC dominates the freelance market. The BBC, however, is required to use a certain amount of material produced by independent producers, and there are increasing numbers of these in the marketplace. There are also many other broadcasting stations in the world. Across the Irish Sea in Dublin Radio Telefis Eireann welcomes talks, short stories, features and plays.Guidelines for radio-writers are available on request. Consider the Commonwealth. In Australia, for instance, there is much more radio at every level than there is in the UK. The Australian Broadcasting Corporation provides television and radio programmes in the national broadcasting service and operates Radio Australia.While ABC radio is interested mainly in contributors with an Australian background, new material of high quality from overseas sources will be considered, submitted either in script or taped form. Radio New Zealand has three public radio networks, of which one is commercial, and a limited short-wave service directed primarily to the Southwest Pacific and Southeastern Australia. New Zealanders are enthusiastic gardeners and deeply interested in anything to do with the countryside. They have been among the most devoted listeners to *The Archers*. Radio plays an important part in the cultural and educational life of India.

Study the list of addresses at the end of this book for other possible markets. Wherever you live in the world you are within reach of radio. Explore the air waves and see how many different stations you can hear. Listen to the sort of material they broadcast, identify a programme you enjoy, and think what sort of a contribution you might make yourself. Follow this up by writing to the station concerned and asking for information about their schedules. They will probably respond with publicity material which will give you some names of producers, executives and presenters. When you have a proposal to put forward you can then address it to someone by name, rather than sending it off into the impersonal blue.

It is essential to study your market, and aim your work carefully at a target slot. The BBC, for example, is an enormous organisation and the programme side is divided into many different sections, which may supply material to any or all of its five main networks. It is not enough to address your script BBC, LONDON and hope that they will find the right destination for it. The *Radio Times* will give you names of producers and editors and a clue as to where different programmes were originated. Different BBC Regions tend to develop their own special areas of excellence. BBC Bristol has become renowned in the field of wild life and natural history; BBC Manchester has an outstanding record in bringing forward new playwrights; BBC Birmingham has always had a strong interest in farming.

National and Regional Production Centres, as well as originating their own local material, are often called upon for productions with specialised requirements. For example, a play which needs a Scottish or Welsh cast may be sent to Radio

87

Scotland or Radio Wales for production, even though it was originally submitted to the Drama Department in London. There is thus a two-way traffic between London and the various production centres, and if you live out of London it may be advantageous to send your script to a local producer.

Local Radio stations are a good deal smaller and simpler in their organisation. They usually have key members of staff who take responsibility for broad areas of programme material. There will be a News Editor, a Sports Editor, perhaps an Educational Producer, and so on. They may or may not be people you hear on the air. A telephone call will give you the name of the right person to approach with a script or a programme idea.

The pattern of local radio programming is built on 'sequences', chunks of time in which a presenter sits at the microphone and introduces music, phone-ins, news, interviews and all sorts of miscellaneous items in a continuous 'seamless' flow. Few contributions last longer than three or four minutes. If you can offer interesting material which will fit in with the style of the station they will be delighted to hear from you. There may be little or no payment, but it will give you a chance to build up a track record. If, when you send a script or an idea to a national network, you can say in your covering letter that you have been working for local radio, that will be evidence of serious commitment, and may help to open a door for you. Voluntary work with Hospital Broadcasting, or Talking Newspapers for the Blind can also help to give you valuable experience.

Copyright

There is no copyright in ideas. What is more, there is no copyright in a title, although there are occasions when the use of a title can be restrained. If you discuss your creative thoughts with other people they are perfectly free to make what use they like of them. The moral of this is that you should not talk about your ideas, but write them down. Once you have given your inspiration written form as a script or a programme format, that expression of your idea is protected by copyright, and it is illegal to make use of it without your agreement. You do not need to complete any formalities to obtain this protection in the UK, or in any country which is a member of the Berne Copyright Union. If at the end of your work you add the notice © followed by your name and the year of completion your script will be protected in all the countries which belong to the Universal Copyright Convention. Copyright law is very complex, and a comprehensive article on the subject is included in the *Writers' and Artists' Yearbook*, published by A & C Black. The Society of Authors also publishes a 'Quick Guide' to copyright and moral rights which is free to members.

There is a fair amount of evidence for the existence of a climate of ideas, which leads to several people thinking along the same lines simultaneously. It is hard to prove who had an idea first, unless a dated script is there to refer to. In order to prove when you submitted your play/format/sketch, you can if you like place a sealed copy in the care of your bank, and obtain a dated receipt for it, or post a copy to yourself at the same time as you despatch it to the broadcasting company. Plagiarism is difficult to prove, but notable actions at law have been brought and won. If you belong to either the Society of Authors or the Writers' Guild they will advise you if you have a case and help you to fight it.

When a company pays for your work it only buys a licence to broadcast it the number of times specified in the contract. The copyright remains your property. If, for example, one of your short stories is accepted for broadcasting. You are perfectly free to sell the serial rights to a magazine, to adapt it as a play for radio, television or the theatre, or to make whatever further use you choose of your own copyright material. Recycling of previously written material can be profitable, and for this reason writers should never throw anything away. An idea may fail at first because the moment is not right for it. Two or three years later the situation may be different. Producers and editors change, and so does the climate of ideas. A word of warning, though: the BBC keeps a comprehensive record of all playscripts ever submitted, with comments. So if you want to have another go with one that has been rejected, rework it thoroughly and give it a fresh title before you send it in again.

Fees

What can you expect to earn? That depends who you are selling to. In Britain the main purchaser of freelance scripted material is the BBC. BBC producers do not talk money. That task is delegated to administrative departments which deal with contracts and copyright. The producer will send a requisition to the appropriate department saying that he wants to commission you, say, to write and deliver a 5 minute talk on brass monkeys. The talks bookings department will then offer you a contract based on a scale of fees agreed with the Writers' Guild and the Society of Authors. You can either accept this, or if you are dissatisfied argue for more money, without sullying relations with your producer. Ideally contracts should be received before the work is done, and certainly before the broadcast takes place, but in the case of topical material this often doesn't happen. Be wary of something called a short talks contract. If you sign it you will not be entitled to any repeat fees however many times the material is used on however many of the BBC's services. It is a form of contract intended for short contributions likely to be of ephemeral interest, and not exceeding an airtime of 10 minutes, for which you will not be expected to have undertaken any research.

Below is a summary of the principle agreed fee scales in force in 1996. Fees are revised regularly, so these figures can be regarded only as an indication.

BBC rates in force 1996

Domestic Radio Drama

		Established writer	Beginner
Original drama (per minute)		£57.38	£37.82
Dramatisations	65%	£37.43	£24.58
	75%	£43.18	£28.37
	85%	£48.94	£32.15

Attendance payment: There is a single payment of £33.87 per production to cover a single attendance which a writer may make at a rehearsal or recording. Further attendances made at the producer's request will be paid at the same rate.

World Service Radio Drama

		Established writer	Beginner
Original drama		£33.87	£22.25
Dramatisations	65%	£22.01	£14.46
	75%	£25.40	£16.69
	85%	£28.79	£18.91

Abridgements

	Established writer	Beginner
Suggested rate (per minute)	£6.77	£4.45

BBC talks and features
These rates have applied since May 1995.

Talks requisition contracts

Interviews
The fees for interviews with an airtime exceeding 10 minutes are negotiable above a minimum of £64.00 for professional broadcasters. (See short talks rates below for short interviews).

Features/Documentaries
The normal rate for professional broadcasters is £171.50 for up to 7 minutes, and £24.50 per minute thereafter. The rate covers presentation, linking, scripting, interviewing and setting up of

interviews, editing, research and all other services required by the BBC to complete the feature.

Note: Talks contributions for one National Region only may be contracted at two-thirds of the full rate.

Script and read
Professional writers and broadcasters: £18.50 per minute.
Non-professionals: £10.00 per minute.
A lower rate of £6.00 per minute may be paid to non-professionals in one national region only. The minimum fee is 2 minutes at the appropriate rate.

Script only
Professional writers and broadcasters: £14.40 per minute.
Non-professionals: £8.00 per minute.
Note: A lower rate of £5.00 per minute may be paid to non-professionals for broadcasts in one National Region only. The minimum fee is 2 minutes at the appropriate rate.

Illustrated talks
These are straight talks in which extracts of illustrative or archival material are used to convey points which cannot satisfactorily be expressed in the words of the script alone. The rate is £14.80 per minute; the minimum fee is 3 minutes.

Day Rates
As an alternative to engaging a freelance to undertake talks contributions under the normal terms and conditions of Talks contracts, the BBC and the freelance may mutually agree an engagement by the day or half day, subject to a minimum of £102.00 per day, or £51.00 per half day, in Network Radio/World Service, and £74.00 per day, or £37.00 per half day in the national regions but this alternative may only be offered in the case of features with a duration not exceeding 15 minutes. Note that the BBC acquires all rights for all purposes in the freelance's contributions made during the day or half day.

Discussions (Network Radio and World Service Radio)
The scale of fees for unscripted discussions is as follows:

No. of speakers	10'	15'	20–26'	27–35'	36'+
2	£56	£73	£90	£114	£145
3	£55	£69	£84	£108	£136
4	£55	£59	£79	£102	£120
5				£90	£109
6				£79	£103

These rates are intended for guidance and are suggested as appropriate for those who earn their living through the written or broadcast word. The chairman will receive the same as other participants unless there are special reasons for paying more.

BBC Radio Short Talks rates

The use of the Short Talks Contract is limited to unscripted contributions not exceeding an airtime of 10 minutes. It is not used for features, even with an airtime of less than ten minutes. The BBC takes all rights for all purposes. The minimum and also standard fee for up to five minutes airtime for a professional broadcaster (interviewer or interviewee) is £48.00 The standard fee for a non-professional interviewee up to 5 minutes airtime is £29.00.

There are circumstances in which the BBC may not pay a fee, e.g. interviews given in support of a topical or current affairs matter such as an industrialist questioned on his/her business, ordinary members of the public without specialist knowledge, interviewees having an interest to promote or an axe to grind or speaking on behalf of an organisation, an author discussing his/her new book. 'New' is defined as 'broadcasts within three months of publication in hardback and/or paperback in the Domestic Services, or within six months on World Service Radio'. Note that where no fee is paid the BBC claims all rights for all purposes.

Local radio

In local radio producers will usually negotiate fees directly with a contributor. The situation varies considerably in different parts of the country. Some stations, for example, will pay for short stories and poetry, others will not. You may be offered nothing at all beyond charming thanks, cash in the hand to cover expenses when you come to the studio, or a T-shirt with the station logo and a sticker for your car. You may get a formal contract, probably after your contribution has been broadcast. It is up to you to be as business-like as you choose, and to balance the experience of broadcasting and having your material used against the value you place on your time.

Audio-visual scripts

If you become involved in the business world of writing promotional tape-slide scripts, your fee will depend on what the market can stand. You will need to assess how long a particular job will take you, and quote a fee based on a reasonable hourly or daily rate. Be realistic. Think in terms of what sort of annual income you earn, and base your fee on a proportion of that figure. There are no guidelines.

Submitting a script or an idea

There are very few slots for one-off radio talks. These days nearly everything is planned in series under magazine titles such as *You and Yours*, *The Afternoon Shift*, *Womans Hour* and so on. If you have an idea for a contribution to one of these, note the name of the producer or editor (either from closing credits or from *Radio Times*), present your idea in the form of a neatly typed letter, and address it personally to the intended recipient.

You may be telephoned by a producer. The telephone conversation can be a sort of audition, to give the producer some idea of what you sound like, and an impression of your vocal personality. You can, if you like, send a cassette with your letter for the same purpose, but don't send a cassette without a script.

In the case of a larger project, perhaps an idea for a feature or a light entertainment series, it is best to approach a producer with a letter of enquiry and an outline of your proposal before putting in a lot of work. If your idea is liked you may be encouraged to develop it more fully.

A newcomer is unlikely to be commissioned to write a full-length drama on the basis of a synopsis and a few pages of dialogue, so if your ambition is to write radio plays you had better submit a complete one. 'They' may not like it, but if they think you have potential you may be asked to write something else.

Scripts should be typed in double spacing with wide margins, on one side of the page only, preferably on A4 paper. There should be a front page with your name, address and telephone number, and this should be repeated on the last page with the international copyright symbol. Fasten the script together with a staple or a paper-clip in the top left-hand corner. If it is bulky you can use a treasury tag and a manila folder, but don't embed it in fancy binding. Attach a brief covering letter and send it with an envelope bearing return postage to your chosen destination. Don't forget to keep a copy.

Covering letters should be brief and to the point. If you have a track record in radio or any other writing field, say so, but don't include an autobiography. Something like this will do:

Melissa Agnew
Radio Drama Producer
BBC North
PO Box 27
Oxford Road
Manchester M60 1SJ

Dear Melissa Agnew,
I am enclosing the script of a radio play which I hope may be suitable for the Thursday afternoon play slot on Radio 4. The action takes place in Bangla Desh, where I lived for some years. Since I now live in Yorkshire I am sending the script to you at BBC North for consideration.
Several short stories and a novel of mine have been published, but this is the first time I have written for radio.
Yours sincerely

William Hopeful

Full details of the current slots for radio drama are given in 'Notes for Writers and Commissioning of Radio Drama on BBC Radio' available from the BBC Radio Drama department. Each slot calls for a play with different characteristics, and probably a different length. Before sending off your script be sure which slot you are aiming at and tailor it accordingly. It is a good idea to enclose a stamped self-addressed postcard, so that the recipient can acknowledge receipt of your script. The BBC usually does this, but not everyone is so scrupulous, and it is comforting to have proof that your script actually arrived as you settle down to wait for a response.

How long should you expect to wait? On average up to three months. If after that time you have heard nothing you can reasonably send a written enquiry. Don't telephone. Hopeless scripts get rejected more quickly than promising ones, so no news can be good news.

You may, of course, choose to send your proposal to an independent production company. It has been suggested that independent radio drama producers are 'more likely to use established radio writers than new ones, more likely to offer adaptations than original works, and more likely to offer formulas chosen for the chance of re-commissioning than for their originality' (Michael Cameron, Writers Guild Newsletter, August 1996). There are, however, some addresses in Appendix II.

Persistence

Finally, the most valuable quality any writer can have in breaking into a new market is persistence. If at first you don't succeed, try, try again – and again. Be ruthless in analysing why your first submission was rejected. Put it away for six months and write something else. Then have a fresh look at the first effort and see if the lapse of time has given you some new insights. And when you do succeed, keep up the pressure. You have a foot in the door of a highly competitive business, and people will forget about you if you don't keep reminding them. Persistence and staying power win through in the end. Good luck!

Appendix 1: Booklist

BBC Annual Report and Handbook (yearly in summer)
BBC Childrens Hour: A Celebration of those Magical Years,
Wallace Grevatt (The Book Guild Ltd of Lewes)
British Radio Drama, John Drakakis (Cambridge University
Press)
Broadcast Journalism – Techniques of Radio and TV News,
Andrew Boyd (Focal Press, 3rd edition 1994)
Chatterboxes: My Friends the Commentators, Brian Johnson
(Methuen)
Complete Plain Words, The, Sir Ernest Gowers, revised by Sidney
Greenbaum and Janet Whitcut (HMSO 1986)
History of Broadcasting in the United Kingdom, The (4 vols.)
Asa Briggs (OUP)
How Plays are Made, Stuart Griffiths (Heinemann Educational)
How to get into Radio, Bernie Simmons (How To Books)
How to write Comedy, Brad Ashton (Elm Tree Books)
In a Class of its Own – BBC Education 1924–1994, John Cain
and Brian Wright (BBC)
Making it as a Radio or TV Presenter, Peter Baker (Piatkus)
Making Radio, Michael Kaye and Andrew Popperwell (Broadside
Books)
Media Guide, The (a *Guardian* book)
Notes on Radio Drama leaflet available on request from BBC
Radio Drama Department.
Passion for Radio, A, edited by Bruce Girard (Black Rose
books)
*Portable Recording – a guide to recorders, microphones and
accessories* Ian Betson (Andrew Bantock Associates)
Radio Authority Annual Report and Financial Statement (yearly
in spring)
Radio Handbook, The, Pete Wilby and Andy Conroy (Routledge
1994)
Radio Production, Robert McLeish (Focal Press, 3rd edition
1994)

Research for Writers, Ann Hoffmann (A & C Black)
Spoken Word, The, a BBC Guide, R.W. Burchfield (BBC)
Way to Write Radio Drama, The, William Ash (Elm Tree Books)
Writers' and Artists' Yearbook (A & C Black, published annually)
Writing for BBC Light Entertainment leaflet available on request from BBC Light Entertainment Department

Some published scripts

Postscripts 1940, J. B. Priestley (Heinemann)

The Man Born to be King, a play cycle written on the life of our Lord and Saviour Jesus Christ, Dorothy L. Sayers (Gollancz)

Six Plays for Radio:
Mathry Beacon
*The Disagreeable Oyster**
Without the Grail
*Under the Loofah Tree**
Unman Wittering and Zigo
Before the Monday   Giles Cooper (BBC)

Best Radio Plays of 1978:
Is it Something I Said? Richard Harris
Episode on a Thursday Evening, Don Haworth
Remember Me, Jill Hyem
Halt! Who Goes There? Tom Mallin
Daughters of Men, Jennifer Phillips
Polaris, Fay Weldon   (Methuen)

Best Radio Plays of 1979:
Typhoid Mary, Shirley Gee
I Never Killed my German, Carey Harrison
Heaven Scent, Barrie Keeffe
Coxcomb, John Kirkmorris
Attard in Retirement, John Peacock
The Child, Olwen Wymark   (Methuen)

Best Radio Plays of 1981:
The Jumping Mimuses of Byzantium, Peter Barnes
Talk of Love and War, Don Haworth
Family Voices, Harold Pinter
Beef, David Pownall
The Dead Image, J. P. Rooney
The Biggest Sandcastle in the World, Paul Thain   (Methuen)

Best Radio Plays of 1982:
Watching the Plays Together, Rhys Adrian
The Old Man Sleeps Alone, John Arden
Hoopoe Day, Harry Barton
Invisible Writing, Donald Chapman
The Dog It Was That Died, Tom Stoppard
Autumn Sunshine, William Trevor   (Methuen)

Best Radio Plays of 1983:
Time Slip, Wally K. Daly
Never in My Lifetime, Shirley Gee
The Angels They Grow Lonely, Gerry Jones
No Exceptions, Steve May
Scouting for Boys, Martyn Read   (Methuen)

Best Radio Plays of 1984:
Who is Sylvia? Steven Dunstone
Transfigured Night, Robert Ferguson
Daybreak, Don Haworth
The Wasted Years, Caryl Phillips
Swimmer, Christopher Russell
Temporary Shelter, Rose Tremain   (Methuen)

Best Radio Plays of 1985:
Outpatient, Rhys Adrian
King Canute, Barry Collins
Three Attempted Acts, Martin Crimp
Ploughboy Monday, David Pownall
Menocchio, James Saunders
Hiroshima: The Movie, Michael Wall   (Methuen)

Giles Cooper Award Winners 1988 (Methuen)

Giles Cooper Award Winners 1989 (Methuen)

*The Goon Show Scripts**, Spike Milligan (Woburn Press, 1972)

*More Goon Show Scripts**, Peter Sellers Harry Secombe and
Spike Milligan (Woburn Press 1973, Sphere 1974)

*Round the Horne**, Barry Took and Marty Feldman (Woburn,
1974)

The Itma Years, scripts broadcast between 1939 and 1949, Ted
Kavanagh (Woburn Press 1974, Futura 1975)

* Recordings available. See below.

Cassette tapes and recordings

The BBC markets recordings of many of its programmes under the title 'The Radio Collection'. A copy of the current catalogue can be obtained from Video Plus Direct, PO Box 190, Peterborough, PE2 6UW, *tel* (01733) 230645. You can also order recordings over the telephone, with a credit card.

School Radio Programmes are marketed by BBC Education Sales, White City, London W12 7TS, *tel* 0181–746 1111. Catalogues are available for Primary, Secondary, Adult Education and Language programmes. All school radio programmes are available on cassette at a flat rate of £2.00 per series. This may not apply to programmes broadcast only in Scotland, Wales or Northern Ireland. Your local BBC Education Officer will be able to advise you.

Appendix II: Some Useful Addresses

British Broadcasting Corporation (BBC)

BBC Corporate Headquarters and BBC Network Radio:
Broadcasting House, London W1A 1AA *tel* 0171-580 4468
fax 0171-637 1630

BBC Network Television:
Television Centre, Wood Lane, London W12 7RJ *tel* 0181-743
8000

BBC Worldwide Television and BBC Worldwide Publishing:
Woodlands, 80 Wood Lane, London W12 0TT *tel* 0181-743 5588

BBC World Service:
Bush House, PO Box 76, London WC2 4PH *tel* 0171-240 3436

BBC White City:
201 Wood Lane, London W12 0TT *tel* 0181-752 5252

BBC Written Archives:
Caversham Park, Reading, Berks RG4 8TZ *tel* (01734) 472742

BBC Midlands and East region
Birmingham: Broadcasting Centre, Pebble Mill, Birmingham B5
7QQ *tel* 0121-414 8888
Nottingham: York House, Mansfield Road, Nottingham NG1 3JB
tel (0115) 955 0500
Norwich: St Catherine's Close, All Saint's Green, Norwich,
Norfolk NR1 3ND *tel* (01603) 619331

BBC North region
Manchester: New Broadcasting House, PO Box 27, Oxford Road,
Manchester M60 1SJ *tel* 0161-200 2020
Leeds: Broadcasting Centre, Woodhouse Lane, Leeds LS2 9PN *tel*
(0113) 244 1188
Newcastle: Broadcasting Centre, Barrack Road, Newcastle upon
Tyne NE99 2NE *tel* 0191-232 1313

BBC South region
Bristol: Broadcasting House, Whiteladies Road, Bristol BS8 2LR *tel* (0117) 973 2211
Elstree: Clarendon Road, Borehamwood, Herts WD6 1JF *tel* 0181-953 6100
Southampton: Broadcasting House, Havelock Road, Southampton SO14 7PU *tel* (01703) 226201
Plymouth: Broadcasting House, Seymour Road, Mannamead, Plymouth PL3 5BD *tel* (01752) 229201

BBC Northern Ireland
Belfast: Broadcasting House, Ormeau Avenue, Belfast BT2 8HQ *tel* (01232) 338000
BBC Radio Foyle: 8 Northland Road, Londonderry BT48 7NE tel (01504) 262244

BBC Scotland
Glasgow: Broadcasting House, Queen Margaret Drive, Glasgow G12 8DG *tel* 0141-339 8844
Edinburgh: Broadcasting House, 5 Queen Street, Edinburgh EH2 1JF *tel* 0131-225 3131
Aberdeen: Broadcasting House, Beechgrove Terrace, Aberdeen AB9 2ZT *tel* (01224) 625233
Inverness (Radio Nan Gaidheal): 7 Culduthel Road, Inverness IV2 4AD *tel* (01463) 221711
Orkney: Castle Street, Kirkwall, Orkney KW15 1DF *tel* (01856) 873939
Selkirk: Municipal Buildings, High Street, Selkirk TD7 4BU *tel* (01750) 21884
Shetland: Brentham House, Lerwick, Shetland ZE1 0LR *tel* (01595) 4747
Solway: 'Elmbank', Lovers' Walk, Dumfries DG1 1NZ *tel* (01387) 68008
Stornoway (Radio Nan Gaidheal): Rosebank, Church Street, Stornoway, Isle of Lewis PA87 2LS *tel* (01851) 705000

BBC Wales
Cardiff: Broadcasting House, Llantrisant Road, Llandaff, Cardiff CF5 2YQ *tel* (01222) 572888
Bangor: Broadcasting House, Meirion Road, Bangor, Gwynedd LL57 2BY *tel* (01248) 370880
Swansea: Broadcasting House, 32 Alexandra Road, Swansea SA1 5DT *tel* (01792) 654986

BBC Local radio stations

Local Radio also affords opportunities for writers to submit short stories and plays. A number of stations hold play-writing or short story competitions where the winners have their work broadcast. Others consider original work from local writers. Material should be submitted to the Assistant Editor.

Bedfordshire: BBC Three Counties Radio, PO Box 3CR, Luton, Beds LU1 5XL *tel* (01582) 411000.

Birmingham: BBC Radio WM, Pebble Mill Road, Birmingham B5 7SD *tel* 0121-414 8484

Bristol: BBC Radio Bristol, PO Box 194, Bristol BS99 7QT *tel* (0117) 974 1111

Cambridgeshire: BBC Radio Cambridgeshire, Broadcasting House, 104 Hills Road, Cambridge CB2 1LD *tel* (01223) 259696

Cleveland: BBC Radio Cleveland, PO Box 95FM, Newport Road, Middlesbrough, Cleveland TS1 5DG *tel* (01642) 225211

Cornwall: BBC Radio Cornwall, Phoenix Wharf, Truro, Cornwall TR1 1UA *tel* (01872) 75421

Coventry: BBC CWR, 25 Warwick Road, Coventry CV1 2WR *tel* (01203) 559911

Cumbria: BBC Radio Cumbria, Annetwell Street, Carlisle, Cumbria CA3 8BB *tel* (01228) 592444

Derby: BBC Radio Derby, PO Box 269, Derby DE1 3HI *tel* (01332) 361111

Devon: BBC Radio Devon, PO Box 5, Broadcasting House, Seymour Road, Mannamead, Plymouth, Devon PL1 1XT *tel* (01752) 260323

Dorset: Dorset FM, Portfolio House, Princes Street, Dorchester DT1 1TP *tel* (01305) 269654

Essex: BBC Essex, 198 New London Road, Chelmsford, Essex CM2 9AB *tel* (01245) 262393

Gloucestershire: BBC Radio Gloucestershire, London Road, Gloucester GL1 1SW *tel* (01452) 308585

Guernsey: BBC Radio Guernsey, Commerce House, Les Banques, St Peter Port, Guernsey, CI *tel* (01481) 728977

Hereford and Worcester: BBC Hereford and Worcester, Hylton Road, Worcester WR2 5WW *tel* (01905) 748485

Humberside: BBC Radio Humberside, 9 Chapel Street, Hull HU1 3NU *tel* (01482) 323232

Jersey: BBC Radio Jersey, 18 Parade Road, St Helier, Jersey, CI *tel* (01534) 870000

Kent: BBC Radio Kent, Sun Pier, Chatham, Kent ME4 4EZ *tel* (01634) 830505

Lancashire: BBC Radio Lancashire, 26 Darwen Street, Blackburn, Lancs BB2 2EA *tel* (01254) 262411

Leeds: BBC Radio Leeds, Broadcasting House, Woodhouse Lane, Leeds LS2 9PN *tel* (0113) 244 2131

Leicester: BBC Radio Leicester, Epic House, Charles Street, Leicester LE1 3SH *tel* (0116) 262 6688

Lincolnshire: BBC Radio Lincolnshire, PO Box 219, Newport, Lincoln LN1 3XY *tel* (01522) 511411

London: BBC GLR, 35c Marylebone High Street, London W1A 4LG *tel* 0171-224 2424

Manchester: BBC GMR, PO Box 951, Oxford Road, Manchester M60 1SD *tel* 0161-200 2000

Merseyside: BBC Radio Merseyside, 55 Paradise Street, Liverpool L1 3BP *tel* 0151-708 5500

Newcastle: BBC Radio Newcastle, Broadcasting Centre, Barrack Road, Newcastle upon Tyne NE99 1RN *tel* 0191-232 4141

Norfolk: BBC Radio Norfolk, Norfolk Tower, Surrey Street, Norwich, Norfolk NR1 3PA *tel* (01603) 617411

Northampton: BBC Radio Northampton, Broadcasting House, Abington Street, Northampton NN1 2BE *tel* (01604) 239100

Nottingham: BBC Radio Nottingham, York House, Mansfield Road, Nottingham NG1 3JB *tel* (0115) 955 0500

Sheffield: BBC Radio Sheffield, Ashdell Grove, 60 Westbourne Road, Sheffield S10 2QU *tel* (0114) 268 6785

Shropshire: BBC Radio Shropshire, 2–4 Boscobel Drive, Shrewsbury, Shropshire SY1 3TT *tel* (01743) 248484

Solent: BBC Radio Solent, Broadcasting House, Havelock Road, Southampton SO14 7PW *tel* (01703) 631311

Somerset: BBC Somerset Sound, 14–15 Paul Street, Taunton, Somerset TA1 3PF *tel* (01823) 252437

Stoke-on-Trent: BBC Radio Stoke, Cheapside, Hanley, Stoke-on-Trent, Staffs ST1 1JJ *tel* (01782) 208080

Suffolk: BBC Radio Suffolk, Broadcasting House, St Matthews Street, Ipswich IP1 3EP *tel* (01473) 250000

Surrey: BBC Southern Counties Radio, Broadcasting Centre, Guildford, Surrey GU2 5AP tel (01483) 306306

Swindon: BBC Wiltshire Sound, Broadcasting House, Prospect Place, Swindon, Wilts SN1 3RW *tel* (01793) 513626

Thames Valley: BBC Radio Thames Valley FM, 269 Banbury Road, Oxford OX2 7DW *tel* (01865) 311444

York: BBC Radio York, 20 Bootham Row, York YO3 7BR *tel* (01904) 641351

Independent national radio

Virgin Radio, 1 Golden Square, London W1R 4DJ *tel* 0171-434 1215 *fax* 0171-434 1197

Classic FM, Academic House, 24–28 Oval Road, London NW1 7DQ *tel* 0171-284 3000 *fax* 0171-713 2630

Talk Radio UK, 3rd Floor, 76 Oxford Street, London W1N 0TR *tel* 0171-636 1089 *fax* 0171-636 1053

IRN (Independent Radio News), 1 Euston Centre, Euston Road, London NW1 3JG *tel* 0171-388 4558 *fax* 0171-388 4449. National news provider to all UK commercial radio stations, including live news bulletins, sport and financial news, and coverage of the House of Commons.

The Radio Authority, Holbrook House, 14 Great Queen Street, London WC2B 5DG *tel* 0171-430 2724 *fax* 0171-405 7062. Licenses and regulates Independent Radio. Plans frequencies, awards licences, regulates programming and radio advertising, and plays an active role in the discussion and formulation of policies which affect the Independent Radio industry and its listeners.

Association of Independent Radio Companies (AIRC), Radio House, 46 Westbourne Grove, London W2 5SH *tel* 0171-727 2646 *fax* 0171-229 0352. AIRC is the trade association of the commercial radio companies in the UK; non-broadcast companies may also join as associate members.

Independent local radio

Aberdeen: NorthSound One FM and NorthSound Two, 45 King's Gate, Aberdeen AB2 6BL *tel* (01224) 632234

Alton: Wey Valley Radio, Prospect Place, Mill Lane, Alton, Hants GU34 2SY *tel* (01420) 544444 *fax* (01420) 544044

Aylesbury: Mix 96, Friars Square Studios, 11 Bourbon Street, Aylesbury, Bucks HP20 2PZ *tel* (01296) 399396 *fax* (01296) 398988

Ayr: West Sound, Radio House, 54A Holmston Road, Ayr KA7 3BE *tel* (01292) 283662 *fax* (01292) 283665

Bedford: Chilton Radio East and Chilton Radio SuperGold East, Broadcast Centre, Goldington Road, Bedford, Beds MK40 3LS *tel* (01234) 272400 *fax* (01234) 218580

Belfast: 96.7 BCR, Russell Court, Claremont Street, Lisburn Road, Belfast, Northern Ireland BT9 6JX *tel* (01232) 438500 *fax* (01232) 230505

Belfast: Downtown Radio/Cool FM, Kiltonga Industrial Estate, Newtownards, Co. Down, Northern Ireland BT23 4ES *tel* (01247) 815555 fax (01247) 818913

Birmingham: 96.4FM BRMB/XTRA-AM, Radio House, Aston Road North, Birmingham B6 4BX *tel* 0121-359 4481 *fax* 0121-359 1117

Birmingham: Choice FM, 95 Broad Street, Birmingham B15 1AU *tel* 0121-616 1000 *fax* 0121-616 1011

Birmingham: Radio XL 1296 AM, KMS House, Bradford Street, Birmingham B12 0JD *tel* 0121-753 5353 *fax* 0121-753 3111

Blackpool: Radio Wave, 965 Mowbray Drive, Blackpool, Lancs FY3 7JR *tel* (01253) 304965 *fax* (01253) 301965

Borders: Radio Borders, Tweedside Park, Galashiels TD1 3TD *tel* (01896) 759444 *fax* (01896) 759494

Bournemouth: Two Counties Radio, 5 Southcote Road, Bournemouth, Hants BH1 3LR *tel* (01202) 294881 *fax* (01202) 299314

Bradford: Sunrise FM, 30 Chapel Street, Little Germany, Bradford BD1 5DN *tel* (01274) 735043 *fax* (01274) 728534

Bradford/Huddersfield & Halifax: The Pulse, Forster Square, Bradford BD1 5NE *tel* (01274) 731521 *fax* (01274) 392031

Brighton: Festival Radio, 6B Steine Gardens, Brighton, East Sussex BN2 1WB *tel* (01273) 777373 *fax* (01273) 205585

Brighton: South Coast Radio, Radio House, PO Box 2000, Brighton, East Sussex BN14 2SS *tel* (01273) 430111 *fax* (01273) 430098

Brighton: Southern FM, Radio House, PO Box 2000, Brighton, East Sussex BN41 2SS *tel* (01273) 430111 *fax* (01273) 430098

Bristol: GWR Radio, PO Box 2000, Bristol BS99 7SN *tel* (0117) 984 3200 *fax* (0117) 984 3202

Bury St Edmunds: SGR-FM, PO Box 250, Bury St Edmunds, Suffolk IP33 1AD *tel* (01473) 461000 *fax* (01473) 741200

Cambridge & Newmarket: Q 103 FM, PO Box 103, The Vision Park, Chivers Way, Histon, Cambridge CB4 4WW *tel* (01223) 235255 *fax* (01223) 235161

Cardiff & Newport: Red Dragon FM, West Canal Wharf, Cardiff CF1 5XJ *tel* (01222) 384041 *fax* (01222) 384014

Cardiff & Newport: Touch AM, PO Box 99, Cardiff CF1 5YJ *tel* (01222) 273878 *fax* (01222) 84014

Carlisle: CFM, PO Box 964, Carlisle, Cumbria CA1 3NG *tel* (01228) 818964

Central Scotland: SCOT FM, Central Radio Scotland Ltd, Number 1, Albert Quay, Leith, Edinburgh EH6 7DN *tel* 0131-554 2266 *fax* 0131-554 2266

Ceredigion: Radio Ceredigion, Yr Hen Ysgol Cymraeg, Ffordd Alexandra, Aberystwyth, Dyfed SY23 1LF *tel* (01970) 627999

Channel Tunnel: Channel Travel Radio, Eurotunnel, UK Terminal, PO Box 2000, Folkestone, Kent CT18 8XY *tel* (01303) 283873 *fax* (01303) 283874

Cheltenham: Cheltenham Radio, Radio House, PO Box 99, Cheltenham, Glos GL53 7YX *tel* (01242) 261555

Chichester, Bognor Regis & Littlehampton: Spirit FM, 9–10 Dukes Court, Bognor Road, Chichester, West Sussex PO19 2FX *tel* (01243) 773600 *fax* (01243) 786464

Colchester: SGR Colchester, Abbeygate Two, 9 Whitewell Road, Colchester, Essex CO2 7DE *tel* (01206) 575859 *fax* (01206) 561199

Cornwall/Plymouth/West Devon: Pirate FM102, Carn Brea Studios, Wilson Way, Redruth, Cornwall TR15 3XX *tel* (01209) 314400 *fax* (01209) 314345

Coventry: Mercia FM and Mercia Classic Gold 1359, Hertford Place, Coventry CV1 3TT *tel* (01203) 868200 *fax* (01203) 868202

Coventry: KIX 96, Ringway House, Hill Street, Coventry CV1 4AN *tel* (01203) 525656 *fax* (01203) 551744

Darlington & Newport Aycliffe: A1 FM, Radio House, 11 Woodland Road, Darlington, Co. Durham DL3 7BJ *tel* (01325) 381032 *fax* (01325) 461235

Derby: Ram FM, The Market Place, Derby DE1 3AA *tel* (01332) 292945 *fax* (01332) 292229

Dumfries: West Sound, Campbell House, Bankend Road, Dumfries DG1 4TH *tel* (01387) 250999 *fax* (01387) 265629

Dumfries: West Sound, Campbell House, Bankend Road, Dumfries DG1 4TH tel (01387) 250999 fax (01387) 265629

Dundee/Perth: Radio Tay AM (PO Box 123), Tay FM (PO Box 1028), 6 North Isla Street, Dundee DD1 9UF *tel* (01382) 200800 *fax* (01382) 593252

Eastbourne/Hastings: Southern FM, PO Box 2000, Brighton, East Sussex BN41 2SS *tel* (01273) 430111 *fax* (01273) 430098

Edinburgh, Forth FM, Forth House, Forth Street, Edinburgh EH1 3LF *tel* 0131-556 9255

Edinburgh: Max AM, Forth House, Forth Street, Edinburgh EH1 3LF *tel* 0131-556 9255 *fax* 0131-558 3277

Exeter/Torbay: Gemini Radio, Hawthorn House, Exeter Business Park, Exeter, Devon EX1 3QS *tel* (01392) 444444 *fax* (01392) 444433

Fort William: Nevis Radio, Inverlochy, Fort William, Inverness-shire PH33 6LU *tel* (01397) 700007 *fax* (01397) 701007

Glasgow: Clyde 1 FM and Clyde 2, Clydebank Business Park, Clydebank, Glasgow G81 2RX *tel* 0141-306 2200 *fax* 0141-306 2265

Gloucester & Cheltenham: Severn Sound, Broadcast Centre, Southgate Street, Gloucester GL1 2DQ *tel* (01452) 423791 *fax* (01452) 529446

Guernsey: Island FM, 12 Westerbrook, St Sampson, Guernsey GY2 4QQ, Channel Islands *tel* (01481) 42000 *fax* (01481) 49676

Guildford & Haslemere: Radio Mercury FM West, The Friary, PO Box 964, Guildford, Surrey *tel* (01483) 451964 *fax* (01483) 31612

Guildford, Haslemere, Reigate & Crawley: Mercury Extra AM, Broadfield House, Brighton Road, Crawley, West Sussex RH11 9TT *tel* (01293) 519161 *fax* (01293) 560927. Broadcasting to Surrey, Sussex and Hampshire

Harlow: Ten 17, Latton Bush Centre, Southern Way, Harlow, Essex CM18 7BU *tel* (01279) 432415 *fax* (01279) 445289

Harrogate: Stray FM, Stray Studios, PO Box 972, Station Parade, Harrogate HG1 5YF *tel* (01423) 522972 *fax* (01423) 522922

Hereford/Worcester: Radio Wyvern, Barbourne Terrace, Worcester WR1 3JZ *tel* (01905) 612212

High Wycombe: elevenSEVENTY, PO Box 1170, High Wycombe, Bucks HP13 6YT *tel* (01494) 446611 *fax* (01494) 445400 *news fax* (01494) 447272

Humberside: Viking FM, Commercial Road, Hull HU1 2SG *tel* (01482) 325141 *fax* (01482) 587067

Inverness: Moray Firth Radio, PO Box 271, Inverness IV3 6SF *tel* (01463) 224433 *fax* (01463) 243224

Inverurie: North East Community Radio, Town House, Inverurie, Aberdeenshire AB51 0US *tel* (01467) 632878 *fax* (01467) 632969

Ipswich: SGR·FM, Radio House, Alpha Business Park, Whitehouse Road, Ipswich IP1 5LT *tel* (01473) 461000 *fax* (01473) 741200

Isle of Wight: Isle of Wight Radio, Dodnor Park, Newport, Isle of Wight PO30 5XE *tel* (01983) 822557 *news tel* (01933) 821777 *fax* (01983) 821690

Jersey: Channel 103, 6 Tunnell Street, St Helier, Jersey JE2 4LU, Channel Islands *tel* (01534) 888103

Kettering: KCBC Radio, PO Box 1584, Kettering, Northants NN16 8PU *tel* (01536) 412413 *fax* (01536) 517390

King's Lynn: KL·FM96·7, PO Box 77, 18 Blackfriars Street, King's Lynn, Norfolk PE30 1NN *tel* (01553) 772777 *fax* (01553) 767200

Leeds/Wakefield/West Yorkshire: Radio Aire FM/Magic 828, PO Box 2000, 51 Burley Road, Leeds LS3 1LR *tel* (0113) 245 2299 *fax* (0113) 242 1380 *news fax* (0113) 242 3985

Leicester: Leicester Sound FM, Granville House, Granville Road, Leicester LE1 7RW *tel* (0116) 256 1300 *fax* (0116) 256 1303

Leicester: Sabras Sound, Radio House, 63 Melton Road, Leicester LE4 6PN *tel* (0116) 261 0666 *fax* (0116) 266 7776

Lincoln: Lincs FM, Witham Park, Waterside South, Lincoln LN5 7JN *tel* (01522) 549900 *fax* (01522) 549911

Liverpool: Radio City, 8 Stanley Street, Liverpool L1 6AF *tel* 0151-227 5100 *newsdesk tel* 0151-471 0216 *fax* 0151-471 0333

London (General and Entertainment Service): Capital Radio, Euston Tower, London NW1 3DR *tel* 0171-608 6080 *fax* 0171-387 2345

London (Brixton): Choice FM, 16–18 Trinity Gardens, London SW9 8DP *tel* 0171-738 7969

London (Haringey): London Greek Radio, Florentia Village, Vale Road, London N4 1TD *tel* 0181-800 8001 *fax* 0181-800 8005

London, Greater: Country 1035, PO Box 1035, London SW6 3QQ *tel* 0171-384 1175 *fax* 0171-384 1177

London, Greater: Festival Radio, Universal House, 251 Tottenham Court Road, London W1P 9AD *tel* 0171-580 5668 *fax* 0171-580 5669

London, Greater: 106·2 Heart FM, The Chrysalis Building, Bramley Road, London W10 6SP *tel* 0171-221 2213

London, Greater: J FM, 26/27 Castlereagh Street, London W1H 6DJ *tel* 0171-706 4100 *fax* 0171-723 9742

London, Greater: Kiss 100 FM, Kiss House, 80 Holloway Road, London N7 8JG *tel* 0171-700 6100 *fax* 0171-700 3979

London, Greater: London News 97·3FM and London News Talk 1152AM, 72 Hammersmith Road, London W14 8YE *tel* 0171-973 1152 *fax* 0171-973 8833

London Greater: Melody FM, 180 Brompton Road, London SW3 1HF *tel* 0171-581 1054 *fax* 0171-581 7000

London, Greater: Premier Radio, Glen House, Stag Place, London SW1E 5AG *tel* 0171-233 6705 *fax* 0171-233 6706

London, Greater: Spectrum Radio, 80 Silverthorne Road, Battersea, London SW8 3XA *tel* 0171-627 4433 *fax* 0171-627 3409

London, Greater: Sunrise Radio 1458AM, Sunrise House, Sunrise Road, Southall, Middlesex UB2 4AU *tel* 0181-574 6666 *fax* 0181-813 9800

London, Greater: Virgin Radio London, 1 Golden Square, London W1R 4DJ *tel* 0171-434 1215 *fax* 0171-434 1197

London, Greater: Viva! 963 AM, Golden Rose House, 26–27 Castlereagh Street, London W1H 6DJ *tel* 0171-706 9963 *fax* 0171-723 9742

Londonderry: Q102·9 FM, The Old Waterside, Railway Station, Duke Street, Waterside, Londonderry, Northern Ireland BT47 1DH *tel* (01504) 44449

Ludlow: Sunshine 855, Sunshine House, Waterside, Ludlow, Shropshire SY8 1GS tel (01584) 873795 *fax* (01584) 875900

Luton/Bedford: Chiltern Radio, Chiltern Road, Dunstable, Beds LU6 1HQ *tel* (01582) 666001

Maidstone & Medway/East Kent: Invicta FM and Invicta SuperGold, Radio House, John Wilson Business Park, Whitstable, Kent CT5 3QX *tel* (01227) 772004 *fax* (01227) 771558

Manchester: Fortune 1458, PO Box 1458, Quay West, Trafford Park, Manchester M17 1FL *tel* 0161-872 1458 *fax* 0161-872 0206

Manchester: Kiss 102, Kiss House, PO Box 102, Manchester M60 1GJ *tel* 0161-228 0102 *fax* 0161-228 1020

Manchester: Piccadilly Radio, 127–131 The Piazza, Piccadilly Plaza, Manchester M1 4AW *tel* 0161-236 9913 *fax* 0161-228 1503

Mid Ulster: Townland Radio 828 AM, PO Box 828 Cookstown, Co. Tyrone BT80 9LQ *tel* (016487) 64828 *fax* (016487) 63828

Milton Keynes: FM 103 Horizon, Broadcast Centre, Crownhill, Milton Keynes MK8 0AB *tel* (01908) 269111 *fax* (01908) 564893

Montgomeryshire: Radio Maldwyn (The Magic 756), The Park, Newtown, Powys SY16 2NZ *tel* (01686) 623555 *phone-in tel* (01686) 624756 *fax* (01686) 623666

North Devon: Lantern FM, The Light House, 17 Market Place Bideford, Devon EX39 2DR *tel* (01237) 424444 *fax* (01237) 423333

North East: Century Radio, PO Box 100, Gateshead NE8 2YY *tel* 0191-477 6666 *fax* 0191-477 5660

North Lancashire/South Cumbria: The Bay 96·9 FM, PO Box 969, St George's Quay, Lancaster LA1 3LD *tel* (01524) 848747 *fax* (01524) 848787

North Wales Coast: Marcher Coast FM, 41 Conway Road, Colwyn Bay, Clwyd LL28 5AB *tel* (01492) 534555 *fax* (01492) 535248

North West: Jazz FM, The World Trade Centre, Exchange Quay, Manchester M5 3EJ *tel* 0161-877 1004 *fax* 0161-877 1005

Northampton: Northants Radio, Broadcast Centre, The Enterprise Park, Boughton Green Road, Northampton NN2 7AH *tel* (01604) 792411 *fax* (01604) 721934

Norwich & Great Yarmouth: Amber Radio, PO Box 4000, Norwich NR3 1DB *tel* (01603) 630621 *fax* (01603) 666353

Norwich & Great Yarmouth: Broadland 102·4 FM, St George's Plain, 47–49 Colegate, Norwich NR3 1DB *tel* (01603) 630621 *fax* (01603) 666252

Nottingham: TRENT FM, 29–31 Castle Gate, Nottingham NG1 7AP *tel* (0115) 952 7000

Nottingham & Derby: GEM AM, 29–31 Castle Gate, Nottingham NG1 7AP *tel* (0115) 952 7000 *fax* (0115) 958 8614

Oxford/Banbury: Fox FM, Brush House, Pony Road, Oxford OX4 2XR *tel* (01865) 748787 *fax* (01865) 748721

Paisley: Q96, 26 Lady Lane, Paisley PA1 2LG *tel* 0141-887 9630 *fax* 0141-887 0963

Peterborough: Classic Gold 1332 AM, PO Box 225, Queensgate Centre, Peterborough PE1 1XJ *tel* (01733) 346225 *fax* (01733) 896400

Peterborough: 102·7 Hereward FM, PO Box 225, Queensgate Centre, Peterborough, Cambs PE1 1XJ *tel* (01733) 460600 *fax* (01733) 281445

Pitlochry & Aberfeldy: Heartland FM, Atholl Curling Rink, Lower Oakfield, Pitlochry, Perthshire PH16 5DS *tel* (01796) 474040 *fax* (01796) 474007

Plymouth: Plymouth Sound, Earl's Acre, Plymouth PL3 4HX *tel* (01752) 227272 *fax* (01752) 670730

Portsmouth & Southampton: South Coast Radio, Radio House, Fareham, Hants PO15 5SH *tel* (01489) 589911 *fax* (01489) 589453

Portsmouth/Southampton/Winchester: Ocean FM, Radio House, Fareham, Hants PO15 5TA *tel* (01489) 589911 *fax* (01489) 589453

Portsmouth, Southampton & Winchester: Power FM, Radio House, Whittle Avenue, Segensworth West, Fareham, Hants PO15 5SH *tel* (01489) 589911 *fax* (01489) 589453

Preston & Blackpool: Red Rose Radio, PO Box 301, St Paul's Square, Preston, Lancs PR1 1YE *tel* (01772) 556301 *fax* (01772) 201917

Reading/Basingstoke: 210 Classic Gold, PO Box 2020, Reading, Berks RG31 7RZ *tel* (01734) 254400 *fax* (01734) 254456

Reading/Basingstoke & Andover: 2-TEN FM, PO Box 210, Reading, Berks RG31 7RZ *tel* (01734) 254400 *fax* (01734) 254456

111

Reigate & Crawley: Radio Mercury FM East, Broadfield House, Brighton Road, Crawley, West Sussex RH11 9TT *tel* (01293) 519161 *fax* (01293) 565663

St Albans/Watford: Oasis Radio, Broadcast Centre, 7 Hatfield Road, St Albans, Herts AL1 3RS *tel* (01727) 831966

Salisbury: Spire FM, City Hall Studios, Malthouse Lane, Salisbury, Wilts SP2 7QQ *tel* (01722) 416644 *fax* (01722) 415102

Scarborough: Yorkshire Coast Radio, 62 Falsgrave Road, Scarborough, North Yorkshire YO12 5AX *tel* (01723) 500962 *fax* (01723) 501050

Severn Estuary: Galaxy Radio, Broadcast Centre, Portland Square, Bristol BS2 8RZ *tel* (0117) 924 0111 *fax* (0117) 924 5589

Shaftesbury: Gold Radio, Longmead, Shaftesbury, Dorset SP7 8QQ *tel* (01747) 855711 *fax* (01747) 855722

Sheffield & Rotherham/Barnsley/Doncaster: Hallam FM and Great Yorkshire Gold, Radio House, 900 Herries Road, Hillsborough, Sheffield S6 1RH *tel* (0114) 285 3333/852121 *fax* (0114) 285 3159

Shetland Islands: SIBC, Market Street, Lerwick, Shetland ZE1 0JN *tel* (01595) 695299 *fax* (01595) 695696

Southend/Chelmsford/Harlow: Essex FM, Breeze and Ten 17, Radio House, Clifftown Road, Southend-on-Sea, Essex SS1 1SX *tel* (01702) 333711 *fax* (01702) 345224

Staffordshire & Cheshire: Signal Radio, Stoke Road, Stoke-on-Trent, Staffs ST4 2SR *tel* (01782) 747047 *fax* (01782) 744110

Stirling: Central 103·1 FM, John Player Building, Stirling Enterprise Park, Stirling FK7 7YJ *tel* (01786) 451188 *fax* (01786) 461883

Stockport: Signal Radio Cheshire, Regent House, Heaton Lane, Stockport, Cheshire SK4 1BX tel 0161-480 5445 *fax* 0161-429 7680

Sunderland: Sun City 103·4, PO Box 1034, Sunderland, Tyne and Wear SR1 3YZ *tel* 0191-567 3333 *fax* 0191-567 0888

Swansea: Sound Wave 96·4 FM, Victoria Road, Gowerton, Swansea, West Glamorgan SA4 3AB *tel* (01792) 893751 *fax* (01792) 898841

Swansea: Swansea Sound 1170 MW, Victoria Road, Gowerton, Swansea, West Glamorgan SA4 3AB *tel* (01792) 893751 *fax* (01792) 898841

Swindon/West Wiltshire: GWR Radio, PO Box 2000, Swindon, Wilts SN4 1WQ *tel* (01793) 440300 *fax* (01793) 440302

Taunton & Yeovil: Orchard FM, Haygrove House, Shoreditch, Taunton, Somerset TA3 7BT *tel* (01823) 338448

Teesside: TFM Radio, Yale Crescent, Stockton-on-Tees, Cleveland TS17 6AA *tel* (01642) 615111 *fax* (01642) 674402

Tendring: Mellow 1557, The Media Centre, 2 St John's Wynd, Culver Square, Colchester, Essex CO1 1WQ *tel* (01206) 764466 *fax* (01206) 764672

Thamesmead: RTM (Independent Radio Thamesmead), Thamesmead Town Offices, Harrow Manorway, London SE2 9UG *tel* 0181-311 3112 *fax* 0181-312 1930

Tonbridge, Tunbridge Wells & Sevenoaks: KFM, 1 East Street, Tonbridge, Kent TN9 1AR *tel* (01732) 369200 *fax* (01732) 369201

Tyne and Wear: Metro FM, Long Rigg, Swalwell, Newcastle upon Tyne NE99 1BB *tel* 0191-420 0971 *fax* 0191-488 9222

West Cumbria: CFM, PO Box 964, Carlisle CA1 3NG *tel* (01228) 818964 *fax* (01228) 819444

West Midlands: 100·7 Heart FM, PO Box 1007, 1 The Square, 111 Broad Street, Edgbaston, Birmingham B15 1AS *tel* 0121-626 1007

Weymouth & Dorchester: Wessex FM, Trinity Street, Dorchester, Dorset DT1 1DJ *tel* (01305) 250333 *fax* (01305) 250052

Whitstable: Invicta Radio, PO Box 100, Whitstable, Kent CT5 3YR *tel* (01227) 772004 *fax* (01227) 771558

Windsor, Slough & Maidenhead: Star FM, The Observatory Shopping Centre, Slough, Berks SL1 1LH *tel* (01753) 551016 *fax* (01753) 512277

Wolverhampton & the Black Country/Shrewsbury & Telford: Beacon Radio, 267 Tettenhall Road, Wolverhampton WV6 0DQ *tel* (01902) 838383; 28 Castle Street, Shrewsbury SY1 2BQ *tel* (01743) 232271

Wolverhampton & the Black Country/Shrewsbury & Telford: WABC, 267 Tettenhall Road, Wolverhampton WV6 0DQ *tel* (01902) 838383 *fax* (01902) 755163 or 838266

Wrexham, Chester & Deeside, Wirral and North Wales: Marcher Sound/Sain-Y-Gororau, The Studios, Mold Road, Wrexham, Clwyd LL11 4AF *tel* (01978) 752202 *fax* (01978) 759701

York: Minster FM, PO Box 123, Dunnington, York YO1 5ZX *tel* (01904) 488888 *fax* (01904) 488878

Yorkshire/Lincolnshire: Great Yorkshire Gold, Radio House, 900 Herries Road, Sheffield S6 1RH *tel* (0114) 285 2121 *fax* (0114) 285 3159; Forster Square, Bradford BD1 5NE *tel* (01274) 731521 *fax* (01274) 392031; Commercial Road, Hull HU1 2SG *tel* (01482) 325141 *fax* (01482) 587067.

Overseas Radio and Television Companies

Australia

Australian Broadcasting Corporation, Box 9994, GPO, Sydney, NSW 2001. Manager for Europe: Australian Broadcasting Corporation, 54 Portland Place, London W1N 4DY. Provides television and radio programmes in the national broadcasting service; operates Radio Australia; operates the international television service, Australia Television; and co-ordinates a network of six symphony orchestras and stages concerts throughout Australia.

ABC television restricts its production resources to work closely related to the Australian environment. ABC radio also looks principally to Australian writers for the basis of its drama output. However, ABC radio is interested in reading or auditioning new creative material of a high quality from overseas sources and this may be submitted in script or taped form. No journalistic material is required. Talks on international affairs are commissioned.

ATN Channel 7, Australian Television Network, Amalgamated Television Services Pty Ltd, Television Centre, Epping, NSW 2121 *tel* (02) 877 7777 *telegraphic address* Telecentre, Sydney *telex* AA 20250 *fax* (02) 877 7886. Unsolicited material not accepted.

BTQ Channel 7, Brisbane TV Limited, Sir Samuel Griffith Drive, Mt Coot-tha, GPO Box 604, Brisbane 4001 *tel* (07) 3369 7777 *fax* (07) 3368 2970. *Network director, chilren's programs*: Dina Browne. Children's educational-type series, children's entertainment programmes. Writers should have a thorough understanding of Australian culture.

HSV Channel 7 Melbourne, HSV Channel 7 Pty Ltd, 119 Wells Street, South Melbourne, Victoria 3205 *tel* (03) 697 7777. No unsolicited material accepted.

National Nine Network (TCN-9 Sydney, GTV-9 Melbourne, QTQ-9 Brisbane, NWS-9 Adelaide, STW-9 Perth), c/o 24 Artarmon Road, Willoughby, NSW 2068 *tel* (02) 9906 9999 *fax* (02) 9958 2279. *Network program director*: John Stephens; *network director of drama*: Kris Noble; *network director program development*: David Lyle. Interested in receiving material from freelance writers strictly on the basis of payment for material or ideas used. No necessity for writers to be Australia-based, but membership of the Australian Writers' Guild helpful.

114

Canada
Canadian Broadcasting Corporation, PO Box 8478, Ottawa, Ontario K1G 3J5 *tel* 613-724-1200.

Republic of Ireland
Radio Telefís Eireann, Donnybrook, Dublin 4 *tel* (01) 2083111 *telex* 93700 *fax* (01) 2083080. The Irish national broadcasting service operating radio and television.
Television: Ongoing production of both a rural and an urban drama serial. Treatments and character profiles accepted for one-off drama productions, drama series and situation comedies, preferably set in Ireland or of strong Irish interest, with preferred durations of commercial half hour or hour length. Forwarding of fully dialogued submissions not encouraged. Before submitting material to Current Afairs, Drama, Features or Young People's programmes, authors are advised to write to the department in question.
Radio: short stories (length 13–14 minutes) in Irish or English suitable for broadcasting; plays (running 30, 60 or 90 minutes) are welcomed and paid for according to merit. Guidelines on writing for radio drama are available from the RTE Radio Drama Department, Radio Centre, Donnybrook, Dublin 4.
Independent Radio and Television Commission, Marine House, Clanwilliam Place, Dublin 2 *tel* (01) 6760966 *fax* (01) 6760948,. Statutory body with responsibility for independent broadcasting. At present there are 21 local radio stations operating in Ireland, in addition to one special interest/community station and one Irish language station. During 1995, 11 community and community of interest radio stations came on-air as part of an 18-month pilot community radio project. It is hoped that a new national independent radio station will be in operation towards the end of 1996. The IRTC is currently in the process of negotiations regarding the establishment of a national independent television service.

New Zealand
Radio New Zealand Ltd, PO Box 2092, Wellington, C1 *tel* (04) 474-1555 *telex* NZ31031 *fax* (04) 474-1340. *Chief Executive*: Joan Withers. A 24-hour state-owned radio enterprise, with editorial and programming independence, controlling a NZ-wide group of over 40 commercial/community stations, two commercial networks and two public service non-commercial networks, and a shortwave service directed primarily to the Pacific area.

Television New Zealand Ltd, PO Box 3819, Auckland *tel* (09) 377-0630 *fax* (09) 375-0918. *Chairman*: Norman Geary; *group chief executive*: Chris Anderson. TVNZ is a state-owned enterprise with production facilities in all four main centres. It owns and operates TV ONE, TV2 and subsidiary companies, South Pacific Pictures Ltd, Avalon Studios Ltd, Broadcast Communications Ltd and Horizon Pacific Television, which operates five regional television stations.

South Africa

South African Broadcasting Corporation, Private Bag XI, Auckland Park 2006 *tel* (011) 714-9111 *fax* (011) 714-3106. Operates five national radio networks, eight regional radio services and three television services.

Markets for Radio Programmes

Almondell Productions (1993), 144 Mansefield, East Calder, West Lothian EH53 0JQ *tel/fax* (01506) 881483. *Contact*: David Calder. Scripts for docs and speech-based programmes; no plays.

Boom Media Ltd (1993), 25 Market Place, Halesworth, Suffolk IP19 8DA *tel* (01986) 875000 *fax* (01986) 875050. *Director*: Nick Patrick. Features and docs with an East Anglian bias, sports' features, popular culture, East Anglian drama.

Business Sound Ltd (1989), Unit 9, Bramley Business Centre, Station Road, Bramley, Surrey GU5 0AZ *tel* (01483) 898868 *fax* (01483) 894056. *Managing director*: Michael Bartlett. Ideas and synopses for packages for the corporate training market; docs. No unsolicited material; initial approach by phone, please.

Fast Forward Radio Products (1994), A132, Riverside Business Centre, Bendon Valley, London SW18 4LZ *tel* 0181-875 9999 *fax* 0181-875 0344. *Producer*: Adrian Quine. Travel, music, current affairs.

Festival Radio productions (Level Broadcast Ltd) (1989), 6B Steine Gardens, Brighton, East Sussex BN2 1WB *tel* (01273) 777373 *fax* (01273) 205585. *Director*: Daniel Nathan. Plays, docs and features.

The Fiction Factory (1993), 201 Greenwich High Road, London SE10 8NB *tel* 0181-853 5100 *fax* 0181-293 3001 *e-mail* drama@mill.cityscape.co.uk. *Creative director*: John Taylor. Plays, dramatisations, readings, documentaries, arts features and children's drama mainly for BBC radio (R4, R2, World Service etc). Ideas for all radio genres considered.

The Flying Dutchman Company (1988), 5–7 Hughes Mews, 143 Chatham Road, London SW11 6HJ *tel* 0171-223 9067 *fax* 0171-585 0459. *Partner*: Michael Cameron. Plays, docs and other programmes on all topics.

GRF Christian Radio (1948), 342 Argyle Street, Glasgow G2 8LY *tel* 0141-221 9447 *fax* 0141-332 9187 *e-mail* grf.radio@scet. org.uk *Programme controller*: Brian W. Muir. Docs on ethical/ moral/religious issues; mini-dramas (up to four minutes) on religious themes; one-minute scripts; children's programmes (religious/educational).

Heavy Entertainment Ltd (1992), 208–209 Canalot Studios, 222 Kensal Road, London W10 5BN *tel* 0181-960 9001/2 *fax* 0181-960 9003. *Company directors*: David Roper, Nick St George. Full-length plays, docs and comedy programmes.

Hispania (1993), 17 Montrose Court, Edgware Road, London NW9 5BS *tel* 0181-905 5000. *Head of Hispanic service*: Bruno Giorgi. Short plays and docs suitable for broadcasting in Spanish, so material translated into Spanish an advantage. Scripts for international and national radio competitions.

Mike Hopwood Productions Ltd (1991), Conway House, Cheapside, Hanley, Stoke-on-Trent, Staffs ST1 1JJ *tel* (01782) 201319 *fax* (01782) 289115. *Editor*: Mike Hopwood. Plays, docs, comedy, sopas, light entertainment.

Independent Productions Ltd (1990), 46A Willowtree Road, Hale, Altrincham, Cheshire WA14 2EG *tel* 0161-928 6105 *fax* 0161-928 6105. *Director*: Tony Hawkins. Scripts and ideas for commercials and promotions for independent radio.

IRDP, PO Box 518, Manningtree, Essex CO11 1XD *tel* (01206) 299088. New writing schemes for radio and theatre, and professional independent productions.

Mediatracks (1987), 93 Columbia Way, Blackburn, Lancs BB2 7EA *tel/fax* (01254) 691197. *Contact*: Steve Johnson. Popmusic and general interest docs for BBC local radio network.

Partners in Sound Ltd, 63 Spencer Rise, London NW5 1AR *tel* 0171-485 0873 *mobile* (01973) 221479 *fax* 0171-428 0541/482 2218 *e-mail* @compuserve 74077,2265. *Director*: Ian Willox. Scripts for plays, docs and other programmes.

Planet 24 (1991), Norex Court, Thames Quay, 195 Marsh Wall, London E14 9SG *tel* 0171-345 2424 *fax* 0171-345 9400. *Development executive*: Tracey Macleod. Scripts, synopses and ideas for plays, docs and other programmes.

Rewind Productions Ltd (1989), The Media Centre, 131-151 Great Titchfield Street, London W1P 8AE *tel* 0171-577 7770 *fax* 0171-577 7771. *Managing director*: Chris Parry-Davies. Plays, docs, popular and classical music, comedy and game shows.

Saffron Productions Ltd (1985), Craigs End, Stambourne, Halstead, Essex CO9 4NQ *tel* (01440) 785200 *fax* (01440) 785775. *Managing director/executive producer*: Victor Pemberton; *director programmes*: David Spenser. Ideas for one-hour plays, and drama series, serials, docs and other programmes.

ScreenPlay Ltd (1987), 25 Cleveland Road, Brighton, East Sussex BN1 6FF *tel* (01273) 708610 *fax* (01273) 708611 *e-mail* bobshep@pavilion.co.uk *Managing director*: Robert J. Shepherd. Scripts for drama and comedy, particularly series and serials. Unsolicited material occasionally considered. Send synopsis and sample dialogue in first instance; sae essential for return of material.

SH Radio (1988), Robert Symes, Green Dene Cottage, Honeysuckle Bottom, East Horsley, Surrey KT24 5TD *tel/fax* (01483) 283223; Mary-Jean Hasler, 22 Carew Road, Ealing, London W13 9QL *tel* 0181-567 2100. Music series, documentary features and broadcast/non-broadcast commercial material, voice over for films.

Smooth Operations (1992), PO Box 286, Cambridge CB1 4TW *tel* (01223) 880835 *fax* (01223) 881647. *Executive producers*: Nick Barraclough, John Leonard. Scripts and ideas for docs and series with popular music theme.

Soundbite Productions Ltd (1991), 55 Tasman Road, Stockwell, London SW9 9LZ *tel/fax* 0171-274 1349. *Managing director*: Lizzie Jackson. Well-thought-out ideas and research for series and programmes for BBC Radio and World Service. Material only accepted from those with a proven track record in radio or TV.

Splash Sound Productions (1982), 1 Mossley Hill Drive, Liverpool L17 1AJ *tel/fax* 0151-724 5813. Ideas for plays, serials, musical drama and comedy.

Testbed Productions (1992), 10 Margaret Street, London W1N 7LF *tel* 0171-436 0555 *fax* 0171-436 2800. *Directors*: Viv Black, Nick Baker. Docs and other programmes; ideas for interviews, feature series, magazine, plays and panel/quiz games.

Miscellaneous

Broadcasting Standards Commission: 7 The Sanctuary, Westminster, London SW1P 3JS *tel* 0171-233 0544

British Forces Broadcasting Service (BFBS): PO Box 1234, North Wharf Road, London W2 1LA *tel* 0171-724 1234

Community Radio Association: the national membership organisation for community radio broadcasters in the UK. Also hosts the European Secretariat of the World Association of Community Broadcasters (AMARC) *tel* 0114-2795 219

Hospital Broadcasting Association: Staithe House, Russell Street, Falkirk FK2 7HP *tel* (01324) 611996

National Association of Hospital Broadcasting (NAHBO): PO Box 2481, London W2 1JR *tel* 0171-402 8815

Radio Independents Organisation (RADIO): PO Box 2261, London NW1 5DG *tel* 0171-453 1670

The Radio Academy (a professional association for those involved in radio broadcasting) 64 Great Titchfield Street, London W1N 7AH *tel* 0171-255 2010

Society of Authors: 84, Drayton Gardens, London SW10 9SB *tel* 0171-373 6642

Student Radio Association: *tel* 0151-794 1900

The Writers' Guild of Great Britain: 430 Edgware Road, London W2 1EH *tel* 0171-723 8074

Voice of the Listener and Viewer (VLV) (a non profit-making society speaking out for quality in broadcasting): 101 King's Drive, Gravesend, Kent DA12 5BQ *tel* (01474) 352835

Awards open to writers and broadcasters

A large number of organisations sponsor awards for media programmes. These are eagerly sought by all the main broadcasting companies, both BBC and independent. The most prestigious awards for work in radio include the following:

SONY Radio Awards: more than thirteen different categories covering writing, performance, production and contributions to radio in all fields. Dept. SRA, Alan Zafer and Associates, 47-48 Chagford Street London N1 6EB *tel* 0171-723 0106

Prix Italia: best radio drama, music and documentary. RAI, Viale Mazzini 14 00195 Rome *tel* 6 3751 4996

Richard Imison Memorial award: for the first dramatic work by a writer new to radio. Society of Authors, 84 Drayton Gardens, London SW10 9SB *tel* 0171-373 6642

Glaxo Fellowship for British Science Writers: award for script and/or programme on a science subject. Association of British Science Writers, c/o Corp. Commms. Dept., Glaxo Holdings

119

plc, Clarges House, 6-12 Clarges Street, London W1Y 8DH *tel* 0171-493 4060

Glenfiddich Awards: for programmes connected with food and drink. Glennfiddich Awards, 10 Stukely Street, London WC2B 5LQ *tel* 0171-405 8638

The Conoco Jet Media Excellence prize for best radio feature on a motoring subject: Conoco Ltd., Conoco Centre, Warwick Technology Park, Gallows Hill. Warwick CV34 6DA *tel* (01926) 404000

BT Hospital Radio Awards: Hospital Broadcasting Association, Staithe House, Russell Street, Falkirk FK2 7HP *tel* (01324) 611996

Medical Radio Awards: (Medical Journalist Association/Smith Kline Beecham) programmes judged to have made best contribution towards understanding of medical issues. 185 High Street, Stratford, Milton Keynes *tel* (019085) 64623

Writers' Guild Awards: categories include drama, comedy, light entertainment, children's and original play. General Secretary, Writers Guild Awards, 430 Edgware Road, London W2 1EH *tel* 0171-723 8074

Radio Times Comedy and Drama awards: for radio's most promising performer, actor and writer whose work falls in the entry period. Associate Publisher Radio Times, Woodlands, 80 Wood Lane, London W12 OTT

Sandford St. Martin C of E Trust Religious Radio Awards: to promote excellence in religious broadcasting. Church House, Room 644, Great Smith Street, London SW1P 3N *tel* (0171) 222 9011 ext. 474

Commission for Racial Equality Race in the Media awards: recognise contribution to public awareness of race relations in Britain. Drama, current affairs, documentary. CRR, Elliot House, 10/12 Allington Street, London SW1E 5EH

Appendix III

This Gun That I Have in My Right Hand is Loaded
by
Timothy West

ANNOUNCER: Midweek Theatre
(MUSIC and keep under:)
We present John Pullen and Elizabeth Proud as
Clive and Laura Barrington, Malcolm Hayes as
Heinrich Oppenheimer, Diana Olsson as Gerda,
and Dorit Welles as The Barmaid, with John
Hollis, Anthony Hall and Fraser Kerr, in *This
Gun That I Have in My Right Hand is Loaded* by
Timothy West, adapted for radio by H. and
Cynthia Old Hardwick-Box.
**This Gun That I Have in My Right Hand is
Loaded.**
(BRING UP MUSIC THEN CROSSFADE TO
TRAFFIC NOISES. WIND BACKED BY SHIP'S
SIRENS, DOG BARKING, HANSOM CAB,
ECHOING FOOTSTEPS, KEY CHAIN, DOOR
OPENING, SHUTTING)

LAURA: (*off*) Who's that?

CLIVE: Who do you think, Laura, my dear? Your husband.

LAURA: (*approaching*) Why, Clive!

RICHARD: Hello, Daddy.

CLIVE: Hello, Richard. My, what a big boy you're
getting. Let's see, how old are you now?

RICHARD: I'm six, Daddy.

LAURA: Now Daddy's tired, Richard, run along upstairs
and I'll call you when it's supper time.

RICHARD: All right, Mummy.
(RICHARD RUNS HEAVILY UP WOODEN
STAIRS)

121

LAURA:	What's that you've got under your arm, Clive?
CLIVE:	It's an evening paper, Laura.
	(PAPER NOISE)
	I've just been reading about the Oppenheimer smuggling case. (*effort noise*) Good gracious, it's nice to sit down after that long train journey from the insurance office in the City.
LAURA:	Let me get you a drink, Clive darling.
	(LENGTHY POURING, CLINK)
CLIVE:	Thank you, Laura, my dear.
	(CLINK, SIP, GULP)
	Aah! Amontillado, eh? Good stuff. What are you having?
LAURA:	I think I'll have a whisky, if it's all the same to you.
	(CLINK, POURING, SYPHON)
CLIVE:	Whisky, eh? That's a strange drink for an attractive auburn-haired girl of twenty nine. Is there . . . anything wrong?
LAURA:	No, it's nothing, Clive, I –
CLIVE:	Yes?
LAURA:	No, really, I –
CLIVE:	You're my wife, Laura. Whatever it is, you can tell me. I'm your husband. Why, we've been married – let me see – eight years, isn't it?
LAURA:	Yes, I'm sorry Clive, I . . . I'm being stupid. It's . . . just . . . this.
	(PAPER NOISE)
CLIVE:	This? Why, what is it, Laura?
LAURA:	It's . . . it's a letter. I found it this morning in the letter box. The Amsterdam postmark and the strange crest on the back . . . it . . . frightened me. It's addressed to you. Perhaps you'd better open it.
CLIVE:	Ah ha.
	(ENVELOPE TEARING AND PAPER NOISE)
	Oh, dash it, I've left my reading glasses at the office. Read it to me, will you, my dear.
LAURA:	Very well.
	(PAPER NOISE)
	Let's see. 'Dear Mr Barrington. If you would care to meet me in the Lounge Bar of Berridge's Hotel at seven-thirty on Tuesday evening the twenty-first of May, you will hear something to your advantage.

(CROSSFADE TO OPPENHEIMER'S VOICE AND BACK AGAIN IMMEDIATELY) Please wear a dark red carnation in your button-hole for identification purposes. Yours faithfully, H. T. Oppenheimer.' Clive! Oppenheimer! Surely that's –

CLIVE: By George, you're right. Where's my evening paper. (PAPER NOISE AS BEFORE) Yes! Oppenheimer! He's the man wanted by the police in connection with this smuggling case.

LAURA: Darling, what does it all mean?

CLIVE: Dashed if I know. But I intend to find out. Pass me that Southern Region Suburban Timetable on the sideboard there. Now, where are we – (BRIEF PAPER NOISE) Six fifty-one! Yes, I'll just make it. Lucky we bought those dark red carnations. (FLOWER NOISE) There we are. Well – (*stretching for fade*) – Lounge Bar of Berridge's Hotel, here . . . I . . . come . . . (FADE) (FADE IN PUB NOISES. GLASSES, CHATTER, TILL, DARTS, SHOVE-HALFPENNY, HONKY-TONK PIANO, KNEES UP MOTHER BROWN ETC.)

HAWKINS: (*middle-aged, cheeful, Londoner*) Evening, Mabel. Busy tonight, isn't it.

BARMAID: It certainly is, Mr Hawkins. I've been on my feet all evening. (*going off*) Now then, you lot, this is a respectable house, this is. (SINGING AND PIANO FADES ABRUPTLY TO SILENCE)

FARRELL: (*approaching, middle-aged cheerful, Londoner*) Evening, George, what are you having?

HAWKINS: No, no, let me.

FARRELL: Come on!

HAWKINS: Well, then, a pint of the usual. (TILL)

FARRELL: Two pints of the usual, please, Mabel. (MONEY)

BARMAID: (*off*) Coming up, Mr Farrell.

HAWKINS: Evening, Norman.

123

JACKSON:	(*middle-aged, cheerful, Londoner*) Hello there George. What are you having, Bert?
FARRELL:	I'm just getting them, Norman.
JACKSON:	Well, leave me out then, I'm getting one for Charlie Illingworth. Two halves of the usual, Mabel.
BAINES:	(*coming up, middle-aged, cheerful, Londoner*) Evening all.
JACKSON:	Hello, Arnold, haven't see you in ages. (TILL)
BARMAID:	Your change, Mr Farrell. (MONEY)
FARRELL:	Thanks Mabel. Where's Charlie got to? Ah, there you are. Charlie, you know Arnold Baines, don't you?
ILLING:	(*cheerful, Londoner, middle-aged*) Known the old so-and-so for ages. What'll you have?
JACKSON:	No, I'm getting them, what is it?
BAINES:	Oh, I'll just have my usual, thanks.
JACKSON:	Who's looking after you, George, old man? (MONEY)
BARMAID:	There's yours, Mr Hawkins.
HAWKINS:	Bung ho. (TILL)
FARRELL:	Cheers George.
BAINES:	Cheers Norman.
JACKSON:	Cheers Bert.
ILLING:	Cheers Arnold. (TILL)
BAINES:	Well, well, look who's coming over.
ILLING:	Isn't that young Clive Barrington from the Providential Insurance?
BAINES:	As happily married a man as ever I saw.
CLIVE:	(*approach*) Evening Arnold. Evening Bert, Charlie, George. Evening Norman.
BARMAID:)	(Evening Mr Barrington.
FARRELL:)	(Evening Clive.
BAINES:)	(*simul.*) (Long time no see.
JACKSON:)	(Hallo Barrington old lad.
ILLING:)	(How goes it.
HAWKINS:)	(What ho then mate.
HAWKINS:	What are you having?
CLIVE:	A whisky, please.
HAWKINS:	Any particular brand?

CLIVE: I'll have the one nearest the clock.

HAWKINS: Half a minute. There's a bloke over there can't take his eyes off you, Clive. Over in the corner, see him? Wearing a dark blue single-breasted dinner jacket and tinted spectacles. A foreigner, or my name's not George Hawkins.

CLIVE: Yes, by George, you're right, George. Excuse me.
(PEAK CHATTER)

OPPENHEIMER: (*middle-European accent*) So, Herr Barrington, you are here at last. I was becoming impatient.

CLIVE: Well, now I am here, perhaps you would be so good as to explain what the blazes all this is about?

OPPEN: Certainly, but not here. We will go to my place in Wiltshire where we can talk. My car is outside. Come.
(FADE ON PUB BACKGROUND)
(FADE UP CAR NOISE SLOWING, STOPPING, ENGINE TICKING OVER)
Excuse me, Officer.

POLICEMAN: Yes, Sir?

OPPEN: Am I on the right road for Wiltshire?

POLICEMAN: That's right sir. Straight on, then turn left.
(CAR REVS UP, MOVES OFF, CROSSFADE TO CAR SLOWING DOWN ON GRAVEL PATH AND STOPPING. CAR DOOR BANGS EIGHT TIMES. FOOTSTEPS ON GRAVEL. FRONT DOOR CREAKS OPEN. DISTANT PIANO, MOONLIGHT SONATA)

OPPEN: Ah, that is my sister playing.
(PIANO NEARER. THE SONATA COMES TO ITS CLOSE. SUSPICION OF NEEDLE NOISE AT END)

GERDA: Ha! Managed that difficult A flat major chord at last.

OPPEN: Gerda, my dear, we have a visitor. Herr Clive Barrington from the Providential Insurance Gesellschaft. Herr Barrington, this is my sister Gerda.

GERDA: I am pleased to meet you, Herr Barrington. Has Heinrich told you what we have in mind?

OPPEN: Nein, not yet, Liebchen. Herr Barrington, first a drink. Champagne, I think, to celebrate.
(CHAMPAGNE CORK, POUR, FIZZ, CLINK)

125

CLIVE:	Thank you. Now, Mr Oppenheimer, or whatever your name is, don't you think it's time you did some explaining?
OPPEN:	Ja, of course. The stolen diamonds about which your Major Kenwood-Smith has seen fit to call in Scotland Yard –
CLIVE:	Major Kenwood-Smith? You mean the Major Kenwood-Smith who's head of my department at the Insurance Office?
OPPEN:	Right first time, Herr Barrington. As I was saying, the diamonds are safely in my hands.
CLIVE:	What! You mean to tell me –
OPPEN:	One moment, please, let me continue. I intend to return them, but on one condition. Now listen carefully; this . . . is . . . what . . . I . . . want . . . you . . . to . . . do . . . (FADE AND UP) . . . and I think that is all I need to tell you, my dear Herr. Now I must leave you: I have one or two . . . little matters to attend to. (*on mike*) Auf wiedersehen. (DOOR SLAMS IMMEDIATELY SOME WAY OFF)
GERDA:	Won't you sit down, Herr Barrington.
CLIVE:	Thank you, Countess. (SITTING NOISE) Look, I don't know how far you're involved in this hellish business, but I would just like to say how exquisitely I thought you played that sonata just now. It happens to be a favourite of mine.
GERDA:	Ja? You liked my playing, yes?
CLIVE:	Beautiful, and yet . . . no, it would be impertinent of me . . .
GERDA:	Please.
CLIVE:	Well then, if you insist. I though that in the Andante – the slow movement – your tempo was a little . . . what shall I say?
GERDA:	Strict?
CLIVE:	Exactly.
GERDA:	(*coming in close*) I had no idea you knew so much about music.
CLIVE:	Please, Countess, I beg of you. I don't know what kind of a hold that filthy swine your brother has

	over you, and I don't want to know, but you don't belong here. For Pete's sake, why not leave with me now, before it's too late.
GERDA:	Nein, nein, I cannot . . . (*in tears*)
CLIVE:	Why, Countess, why?
GERDA:	I will tell you. It is better that you should know. It all started a long time ago, when I was a little Fraulein in the tiny village of Bad Obersturmmbannfuehrershof, in the Bavarian Alps . . .
	(FADE, BRING UP LONDON TRAFFIC. BIG BEN CHIMES THE HOUR AND THEN STRIKES TWELVE. AS IT STRIKES WE MOVE OUT OF THE TRAFFIC, A CAR STOPS, SQUEAL OF BRAKES, CAR DOORS, FOOT-STEPS, NEWSBOYS, TUGS, BARREL ORGAN, CREAKING DOOR, MORE FOOTSTEPS DOWN A VERY VERY LONG CORRIDOR PASSING OFFICES WITH TYPEWRITERS UNTIL A SMALL DOOR OPENS AT THE END OF THE PASSAGE AND WE MOVE INTO A SMALL ROOM ON THE LAST STROKE OF TWELVE)
POWELL:	Ha! Twelve o'clock already. Morning, Sergeant McEwan. Or perhaps I should say 'Good Afternoon.'
McEWAN:	(*Scots*) Whichever you like, sir!
	(GOOD HUMOURED LAUGHTER)
POWELL:	As a matter of fact, I've been out on a job already this morning. I bet you just thought I'd overslept, didn't you, Sergeant?
McEWAN:	What, you, sir? Hoots, no. Not Detective-Inspector 'Bonzo' Powell, VC, who went over the top at Tobruk; one-time Channel swimmer, and one of the toughest, and at the same time one of the most popular, officers at Scotland Yard here? I should say not, Och.
POWELL:	No, I got a line on our old friend Heinrich Oppenheimer, at long last. Our chap at Swanage says Oppenheimer has a private submarine moored nearby – it's my guess he'll try and get the diamonds out of the country tonight.
McEWAN:	Havers! Where will he make for d'ye ken?

127

POWELL:	I don't know, but it's my guess he'll make straight for Amsterdam. Come on, Sergeant, we're going down to Swanage. And . . . the . . . sooner . . . the . . . better . . . (URGENT MUSIC, THEN FADE BEHIND GULLS, ROWLOCKS, WASH. STUDIO CLOCK SHOULD BE PARTICULARLY NOTICEABLE IN THIS SCENE) (NOTE: ALL THE GERMANS IN THIS SCENE ARE INDISTINGUISHABLE ONE FROM THE OTHER AND INDEED MAY ALL BE PLAYED BY THE SAME ACTOR AS OPPENHEIMER)
LUDWIG:	We are nearly at the submarine now, mein Kommandant.
OPPEN:	Ach, Zehr gut. Tell me once more what you have done with the prisoners; my sister Gerda and that meddling fool Barrington.
LUDWIG:	Karl found them attempting to telephone Scotland Yard from the porter's lodge. They have been tied up and taken on board the submarine half an hour ago.
OPPEN:	That is gut. I will teach the fool Englishman to double-cross me. Achtung! Here we are at the submarine. Karl! Heinz! Kurt! Lower a rope ladder!
KARL:	Ja, mein Kommandant. (FEET ON TIN TRAY)
OPPEN:	It is four o'clock. We will sail immediately. (CHANGE TO SUBMARINE INTERIOR ACCOUSTIC)
HEINZ:	The diamonds are safely locked in your cabin, mein Kommandant.
OPPEN:	Jawohl. Kurt! Heinz! Karl! Prepare to dive! (DIVING NOISES, KLAXON) Set a course for Amsterdam.
KURT:	Steer East North East eight degrees by north. (CRIES OF JAWOHL, ACHTUNG, MIDSHIPS etc.)
OPPEN:	Ludwig!
LUDWIG:	Ja, mein Kommandant.
OPPEN:	Take me to the prisoners.
LUDWIG:	Ja, mein Kommandant. (MORE FEET ON TIN TRAY) They are in the forward hydroplane compartment.

	(DOOR OPENS. FORWARD HYDROPLANE COMPARTMENT NOISES)
OPPEN:	So, Herr Barrington, we meet again.
CLIVE:	You filthy swine, Oppenheimer, you won't get away with this.
OPPEN:	(*becoming slightly manic*) On the contrary, my friend, there is no power on earth that can stop me now. You, I'm afraid, will never reach Amsterdam. There will be an unfortunate . . . accident in the escape hatch.
GERDA:	(*a gasp*) Heinrich! You don't mean . . .
OPPEN:	As for you, my dear sister Gerda . . .
CLIVE:	Leave the girl out of it, Oppenheimer. She's done nothing to you.
OPPEN:	Charming chivalry, my English friend. But it is to no avail. Come.
CLIVE:	All right, you swine, you've asked for it! (BLOW)
OPPEN:	Aargh. Himmel! Karl, Kurt! (RUNNING FOOTSTEPS)
CLIVE:	Ah, would you? Then try *this* for size. (BLOW, GROAN) If *that's* the way you want it. (BLOW, GROAN)
KURT:	Get him, Hans.
CLIVE:	Ah, no you don't. Take *that*. (BLOW, GROAN. A CHAIR FALLS OVER)
GERDA:	Look out Clive. The one with glasses behind you. He's got a gun. (SHOT)
CLIVE:	(*winces*) (ANOTHER CHAIR FALLS OVER) Phew! Close thing, that.
GERDA:	Clive? What happened?
CLIVE:	Just my luck; he got me in the arm. Luckily, he caught his foot on that bulkhead coaming; he must have struck his head on that valve group between the depth gauge and the watertight torpedo door.
GERDA:	Is he – ?
CLIVE:	I'm afraid so. Right, now to get this thing surfaced.
GERDA:	Do you know how?
CLIVE:	It shouldn't be too difficult. Luckily I had a week

on Subs in the R.N.V.R. years ago. (*with pain*)
This right arm being Kaput doesn't help, though.
Right, now, just blow . . . the . . . ballast from
main . . . and . . . number four . . . tanks . . .
adjust the Hammerschmidt-Brucke stabilisers . . .
and up – we – go.
(SUFACING NOISES, SEA. THE CRY OF
GULLS. A FEW BARS OF 'DESERT ISLAND
DISCS' MUSIC. CROSSFADE TO CHATTER,
CLINK OF GLASSES)

LAURA: Have another drink, Sergeant.

McEWAN: Thank you, Mrs Barrington. I'll have a wee drappie.

CLIVE: How about you Inspector?

POWELL: Don't mind if I do, sir. Charming place you have here, if I may say so; and a charming wife to got with it.

LAURA: (*blushing*) Thank you, Inspector.

CLIVE: Well, I don't mind saying, Inspector, there were one or two moments today when I wondered if I'd ever see either of them again.

LAURA: Tell us, Inspector, exactly when was it you came to realise that Major Kenwood-Smith was behind it all?

POWELL: Well, for a long time it had puzzled us that the safe was blown by a left-handed man – Oppenheimer and his henchmen are all right-handed. Luckily one of our chaps noticed Kenwood-Smith signing a cheque with his *left* hand.

CLIVE: Aha.

POWELL: We asked him a few questions, and he broke down and confessed. Sergeant, you can go on from there.

McEWAN: Ay, well, the diamonds aboard the submarine turned out to be imitation. Oppenheimer must have been double-crossed at the last minute, and someone in Berridge's Hotel must have performed the switch.

CLIVE: Great Scott, the barmaid!

POWELL: Right, first time, Mr Barrington. We checked in our archives, and she turned out to have a record as long as your arm. She made a dash for it, but in the end she broke down and confessed.

CLIVE: So everything turned out for the best in the end, eh?

POWELL: That's right sir. And just think, Mrs Barrington, if it hadn't been for young Richard here losing his puppy on Wimbledon Common, none of this might ever have happened.

(YAPPING ON DISC)

RICHARD: Down, Lucky, down!

POWELL: Now then, young pup, none of that gnawing at my trouser leg, or I'll have to take you into custody as well!

(GENERAL LAUGHTER. LIGHT HEARTED ROUNDING-OFF MUSIC AND UP TO FINISH.)

ANNOUNCER: *(spinning it out – the Play has under-run)*: You have been listening to *This Gun That I Have in My Right Hand is Loaded* . . .

Index